I WOULD HAVE
SEARCHED FOREVER

By Sandra Kay Musser

Distributed by
Adoption Awareness Press
A Division of
The Musser Foundation
Cape Coral, Florida 33910

Everything in this book is true and happened exactly as written. However, to insure privacy, many of the names have been changed.

I Would Have Searched Forever
5th Printing

Acknowledgements

Because this is such a personal story, I would like to acknowledge all those special people in my life who have significantly influenced me. Though they are too numerous to mention, they know who they are; I appreciate the constant support as we've traveled this sod together.

I had no idea that preparing a book for publication was such a huge task. I am, therefore, deeply grateful to my friend, John Poole, who believed I had something worth saying, agonized with me as I struggled to say it, and encouraged me through to completion.

To Jim, Linda, Sherri and Steve, my four wonderful teenagers who kept insisting that I let everything else go and finish my book, a great big THANK YOU for prodding me along.

I am indebted to you all for the faith you have placed in me.

This book is dedicated to:

My Mother

who showed me the Way to the Father (John 14:6) and was constant in reminding me that *"All* things work together for good to those who love God."

(Romans 8:28)

and

All Birthparents

who have known the pain of surrendering a child. "Can a woman forget her child, that she should not have compassion on the son of her womb?"

(Isaiah 49:15)

FOREWORD

This was not an easy book to write. It is not simply a book about adoption. It does not present a multitude of facts concerning children and birthparents gathered from the statistical tables of studies done 'somewhere' by 'someone'.

This is the very real story of a very real person. Sandy Musser has opened her life and her heart to us. With courage and candor she has allowed us to see the pain of an unwed teenager's experience, the aching heart of a mother who knows that somewhere in this world there is a child to whom she gave life, a child that she carried in her womb, a child that she knows nothing about.

This is the story of the search for that child. It is the story of a woman who, against hope, believed in hope and received the promise.

It is, however, far more than a narrative. For that reason it will not be an easy book for some to read, for it speaks of issues that are complex and difficult. It raises the question of the rights of birthparents.

"How much should they know about the lives of their children, and when should they know these things, if at all?"

What about the children themselves?

"How important is it that they have an understanding of where they came from? How much of a role does that play in helping them determine who they are?"

And the adoptive parents.

"Are their fears justified? Will the security of millions of homes be torn apart by the possible answers to these and similar questions?"

After reading Sandy's story, you will not have all the answers, but you will understand a point of view. You will see from a perspective that you may not have been exposed to before. How do I know this? It has been my experience. I am the father of six adopted children, and it was not until my conversations with Sandy, and the opportunity to read her manuscript that I began to understand the other side. And maybe, if we all begin to see each other's hurts and fears, a resolution to this serious dilemma may be forthcoming. This book makes a significant contribution toward finding a solution to these questions. I commend it to you highly.

–John M. Poole
Barrington, NJ
May 7, 1979

7

PREFACE

Leaving the hospital that day in July of 1954, I realized that a chapter of my life had just ended and, according to society, it was a chapter which would never be brought to light again. What an understatement! What an impossibility! How does one "forget" giving birth to a child? How can one live as though it never happened? With each event that ends, there is another beginning and so my life of hiding away my secret had just begun. After all — that was what was expected of me. Just forget and start over. Very simple — at least it seemed so for those who made this absurd statement.

In order to help make all this a reality, the law even produces a completely new birth certificate with the names of the new parents so no one need ever know that the child was born to other people. With that done, the game and the drama begins.

In my case the game continued until 22 years later, when by my own decision, I came out of the closet, out of hiding, in order to put some flesh on the old skeleton that had been kept in the dark for too long.

This is the story of one girl's experience, one mother's heartache, and one woman's faith. This is my story.

Sandy Musser

The author is available for speaking engagements. Please write to:

ADOPTION TRIANGLE MINISTRIES
P.O. Box 1860
Cape Coral, FL 33910
813-542-1342

Table of Contents

Section I — Autobiography

No mortal can keep a secret.
If his lips are silent,
he chatters with his fingertips;
betrayal oozes out of him at every pore.

— Sigmund Freud

Introduction – April, 1977

I couldn't believe my eyes. Here I was staring at a piece of paper with a name on it – a name I had longed to know for 22 years – and now here it was – right before my eyes. I could hold the paper in my hand and stare at this name for as long as I wanted.

I did just that! I certainly had the right to after waiting so many years – or did I? Over and over again I repeated the words "I can't believe it, I can't believe it." My dream had finally become a reality, my prayers had been answered. I now knew her name. The name I had longed to know. All the while I stared at the paper, there seemed to be something legally, morally, or socially wrong with my gazing upon it. "Why do I feel this way?" I thought. I was looking at the name of my child whom I had surrendered to adoption many years before, and I was feeling guilty about it! How very crazy! Who laid this heavy burden on me? She was now an adult; why didn't I have the right to know the name of this child who had always remained in my heart? Why couldn't I know how she had fared over the years? Why couldn't I have the assurance that I had done the right thing for her? Hadn't I suffered long enough? Hadn't I done well to keep "the secret" for so long?

The time had now come that I wanted to shout it from the roof-tops – "Hey, I've got a daughter out there somewhere, and I want to know her. I want to see her and tell her why I had to give her up. I want to be able to explain the circumstances surrounding her birth. Please society, tell me I have a right. Don't you see that I've paid my debt; I've served my time? Can't I now be free? Can't I come out of hiding? Can't I reveal the secret that's been eating away at me all these years? Why must you keep heaping this guilt upon me?"

15

Well, my shell has broken and I'm emerging. The light is sifting through and hope is at hand. The light has a way of making one see clearly what could not be seen before. It cuts through the darkness like a sharp blade spreading its beams around for all to see. My night was about to become day. The sunshine is warm and soothing and I'm finding more comfort in it than my life in the cocoon. The protective covering which I had wrapped about me could no longer contain the growth that was going on inside.

As the light shone through, I was able to observe things from a different perspective and to realize that relationships are more important than anything else in life. Certainly they are more important than man-made adoption laws which were created to "protect" people from knowing each other. I find there is a higher law — the law of love. That which says, "If you are suffering pain, I want to help you relieve that pain." If knowing one's past, for whatever reasons, will help, then why not eliminate all the secrecy? Why is it considered such a threat for people involved in the triangle to know one another? Do we possess one another or even think that we can? Do we need to protect one another from knowing about ourselves? Could this be an insecurity within us that causes us to want to reject anything or anyone new coming into our existence?

As I contemplated the enormous problems surrounding the adoption issues, my mind wandered back many, many years to that fateful day in January, 1954.

The Shadows of Childhood

I'll never forget the day mother said she wanted to have a talk with me. It was a cold day in January. She had such a sadness about her and while, subconsciously, I must have known the subject matter to be discussed, I nevertheless was curious at the same time. The innocence of a 15 year old in 1954! As we sat down on the bed in my room, she looked at me and said, "Sandra, Betty Ann (my sister) tells me there is a rumor going around school that you could be pregnant — is it true?" As the butterflies flurried around in my stomach and my mouth became dry, I responded with a simple, "I don't know," while in my mind I was thinking, "Is it possible?" Finally, I uttered a feeble, "I guess so". Then the tears and the outpouring of a mother's heart as she verbally wonders what she did wrong, and the pain in my own heart for the terrible hurt I was causing her. How very difficult to sit and watch your own mother cry and what a revelation! So often parents fail to show their children the deep emotional side of their nature. As children we tend to think that our parents are beyond these feelings. The words continued to flow — my own frustration of not having my "real" father, the fact that Len "really" did love me, the realization that I would have to quit school. Our conversation ended with the decision to visit our long-time family physician to find out for sure if I was pregnant.

The following evening we had an appointment with Doc Callahan, a dear man whom we all loved. He had asked that we come early so he could take us ahead of the other patients. After the examination, Doc asked me to wait in the outer office while he spoke to mother alone. Chills ran through my whole body realizing that this meant what we had suspected was true. I was pregnant. I had celebrated my

15th birthday just two weeks before. I walked straight through the outer office into the coldness of the clear, dark, January night.

As I gazed up into the starlit heaven, I tried bargaining with God once more; promising him that I'd be a "good girl" if I wasn't pregnant. But I knew in my heart that there was no bargaining to be done. Dazedly, I walked. Maybe I could just keep on walking and "disappear". That would save my precious mother the shame she was going to have to bear because of me. It was only a short time before I heard her voice calling my name. I wanted to run away — from her — to her — throw my arms around her and say, "Ma, I'm sorry." But no words came — just tears and her own comforting words that I shall never forget. "Honey, I would go through anything for you, but this is one thing that you've got to go through alone. If there were some way I could go through it for you, I would. I can only stand with you and I will." While a 15 year old teenager appreciates very little, the words of my mother that evening were the most soothing, the most comforting I could have heard. She reminded me of the virtuous woman spoken of in Proverbs — a real jewel — a beautiful gem, full of compassion, love, devotion, and understanding. How I've thanked God many times over for a loving, faithful, and devoted mother at a time when she was needed most — a very tragic time for a young teen in the early '50s.

From the outset of the knowledge of my pregnancy, there was never a question as to the father's identity. We had spent a year and a half in each other's company — hand-in-hand, totally engrossed in each other's lives. A young teenage romance, laughing, teasing, sharing, loving; a year and a half of being wrapped up in the life of the person I loved. As a child of a broken home, I craved that more than anything else. I was resentful and bitter about not having my real father. My stepfather and I did not get along at all. It was not any fault of his, but simply my own refusal to accept him as a substitute father.

I used to hope and pray that somehow, someway, my parents would get back together and we would live happily ever after. I guess every child who finds themselves in a broken home situation has the same hope at one time or another. Mother had left Dad in 1944 — a rebel in her own right for that time period. For years I was the only one in my class whose parents were divorced and I was extremely conscious of it. When I was in second grade, I began using my mother's new married name. The teacher promptly sent a note home asking if my stepfather had adopted me. I'm sure that was the first time I had ever heard the word adopted. I didn't like the idea of having a name different than my mother's so I tried to compensate by using hers. I was told that I was not permitted to do that. I'm not sure how long it took me to understand, but I did knuckle under the pressure of authority and discontinued using my stepfather's name. As a high school student I resented having to tell my friends that my parents were divorced. I can't explain why I had these feelings, but only that I did, and they were very real.

Unfortunately during the rest of my teen years, I never did accept my stepfather. I found that I was able to play one against the other and took advantage of the situation often. My mother always defended me and because of my intense dislike for him, I would manage to get them at odds with one another. I guess I was jealous of "losing" my mother to someone else – especially to another man who was not my father! It was not until after I was married that I could appreciate the responsibility he had assumed and the efforts he made in trying to be a good substitute father.

Well, Doc had verified the fact that I was pregnant. He told mother that as far as he could determine, I would give birth around July 23. Decisions now had to be made as to what would be done with me. Pregnant girls just did not remain in their hometowns in those days. A special Board of Education meeting was held to determine if I would be permitted to remain in school and if so, for how long. Mother had a close friend who was an active member which enabled me to remain in school longer than others might have preferred.

I had been active in sports, hockey, basketball, etc., so I continued to play. Since I had not gained much weight, I was not "showing". However, one day in Home Ec. class, while standing on a table having a skirt pinfitted, I suddenly became very dizzy and slumped over. That day, near the end of March, was my last day in school for my Sophmore year.

Clubs were the "in" thing with girls in those days. We were very clannish and formed our own little elite group. We called ourselves the Silouhettes (a popular song of the day). We purchased jackets with the Silouhette name on the back and our own name on the front and we each carried a membership card which stated that we were a member "in good standing". As the grapevine made its way through the crowd concerning my pregnancy, meetings were held to determine whether I should be permitted to remain in the club. I was well aware that this was going on since sides were being drawn. Some of the girls claimed that their parents would not allow them to continue in the club unless I were put out! At long last, a vote was taken. I lost (or did I really win?). I received a letter stating that I was being kicked out of club because I was no longer a "member in good standing" and I should return my card. As I look back, it seems funny and certainly unimportant, but at that point in my life, it was the most crushing blow I received from my closest peers.

I responded with a letter expressing that I truly hoped none of them would ever have to experience what I was going through. I meant it. I knew that they could not begin to comprehend the fear, the loneliness, and the uncertainty that I was feeling. I doubted that any of them had ever wanted to take their life as I had contemplated at that time. It was not sympathy that I was seeking. It was understanding. There were two or three close friends who stuck by me, jeopardizing their own reputations to associate with me. There were the curiosity seekers who came to visit me at home after I had quit school. Girls who I never associated with came to "befriend" me. Usually just once. I was tutored until the end of May and was able to complete my sophomore year.

When word got around of my pregnancy, my relationship with Len ended quite abruptly. It was suggested to him that he deny paternity. He didn't. Nevertheless, our short-lived love-affair was over — over in reality, but not over in my heart. They say that young teens can't be in love. They call it infatuation. I don't really know. I felt that I loved him with all my being and would have done anything for him. One of my regrets is that I never had the opportunity to find out what it must have been like for him to go through this experience. Was he scared or upset by all the talk? Did he ever cry over the situation? Was he concerned about me? I suspect that the answer is yes to all those questions.

Mother asked if I wanted to get married. She said it was my decision and if I wanted to, she would force the issue. I knew deep down inside that Len did not love me and I was old enough to realize that a forced marriage would not solve anything. We had two more years of school to complete and Len was planning to go to college. I discussed my thoughts with her and it was then that adoption was agreed upon. I was not pressured in any way. I believed it was in everyone's best interest for me to surrender my child. I have never regretted my decision and still think I did the right thing, painful as it was.

Early in June I was shuttled off to a private shelter home. In exchange for my room and board, I would help with the household chores and babysitting. The Brysons were wonderful to me. I was accepted and made to feel very much a part of their family. Prior to being placed in this home, Mother and I had visited some homes for unwed mothers. Neither of us liked what we observed and I guess she just couldn't imagine placing her little girl in a "home" where I'd be just another body.

During the next month and a half I spent the majority of my waking hours helping with housework and babysitting three young children. My room, warm and cozy, was in the basement of the home. I retreated there as often as possible. It was here I listened to my radio and the songs that had special meaning; songs that reminded me of my broken relationship with my first love. Songs like "Cold, Cold Heart", "Someday" and "Cry" by Johnnie Ray, my favorite singer of the day. It was from this room that I followed and cheered on my favorite baseball team, the Philadelphia A's. It was here that I wrote many, many letters to my closest friends and shared with them the depths of my soul. It was in this very room that I talked with God and asked for his forgiveness.

Mother would visit a few times a week. We'd go out and get an ice cream treat, spend a few hours together, and then she'd take me back to my temporary home. Often she would bring Terry, my little sister, who was only 10 months old. Mother had tried for seven years to have a child by her second marriage and finally, at age 40, Terry May arrived. I really enjoyed her and spent a lot of my spare time sewing and making clothes for her. Though we are 14 years apart, we have become very close. We are a lot alike and understand each other well. She recently told me that when she first heard about me having a child at 15, she wondered about the possibility of my being her mother.

Toward the end of June my doctor appointments were scheduled a week apart. These visits were times of mixed emotions. I had a crush on my doctor who looked just like Clark Gable; however, I felt extremely self-conscious being in a roomful of "older" pregnant women. I was quite naturally out of place as their stares reminded me.

Len's birthday was on July 17 – his 16th birthday. I thought it would really be neat if our child were born on his birthday. I had spoken to him on the phone the evening of the 17th and shared my feeling. Sixteen hours later I was in the hospital giving birth to my first child – a child I would not see for 23 years!

It was Sunday morning. I awoke early which was unusual for me! I had a knack for sleeping late. The pains were coming every 20 minutes. I called mother who in turn called the doctor. Mother called back with the message that when the pains were ten minutes apart, we should leave for the hospital. By 8:15 they were ten minutes apart. Mr. and Mrs. Bryson drove me to the hospital.

21

They say ignorance is bliss and that was my experience with childbirth. When they took me into the "prep" room, I remember asking the nurse, "Is this going to hurt?" She was getting ready to shave me! She laughed as she said "This ain't nothing compared to what's ahead!" She wasn't kidding, but I had absolutely no idea what I was in for!

Shortly I was taken into the labor room, put into a crib-like bed and, in between moans and groans, had to give an information report. "What was my name, address, age, occupation, father's name, age, etc.?" It seemed that in no time at all, the pains became severe, one on top of the other and they seemed to last an eternity. I know I wanted to die and cried out that I would. I don't recall being given anything for the pain. I've often wondered if I wasn't permitted to suffer intentionally so I could learn a lesson. That is a judgement on my part, but that's the way I felt. This feeling has been shared by many birthparents. There was one nurse who stayed by my bed and held my hand during the entire labor. I have never forgotten her and would someday like to thank her for the compassion she showed me. I don't remember going into the delivery room or the actual birth. I do recall that when I woke up, I glanced at a clock on the wall which said 2:00. I learned later that I had delivered at 11:45 a.m.

Mother came to see me later that day. The doctor had told her it would be better if she were not there while I was in labor as there wasn't anything she could do. He was right and I was grateful that she did not have to see me in pain. Instead she was in church worshipping the God she loved and praying for her little girl. By the time she got out of church, I had had my baby — mother and child doing fine!

During the time I was in the hospital, I tried to convince, connive, even conjure the nurses into allowing me to see my baby. I never succeeded. I was in a private room and not permitted to leave it. As rebellious a teenager as I had been, I obeyed. I never left the room, though I often peeked out the door to see if I could catch a glimpse of my child. The nurses were all friendly and nice, but I was unable to get any of them to discuss my baby — except that she weighed seven pounds, one ounce, and, of course, was beautiful!

Mother told me that the adoptive parents would be taking her directly from the hospital and that they would name her. I had never been informed that I could have named her. Her original certificate reads "Baby Girl Musser".

A week later I would reenter the world from which I had come; hopefully a wiser, richer person for the experience I had been through. A 15½ year old unwed mother about to converge again into the mainstream of life. Not an easy task! More difficult than I had anticipated. Another month and I would be back to school.

I returned in September of 1954 with mixed emotions. How would I be treated? What would I say? How would I act? One of the fellows in our class had a party shortly after school started to which I was invited. Ironically, he was an adoptee. His mother received calls from some of the girls' mothers asking if I would be attending. When she told them I would be, they said that their daughters could not come. I realize now that Bill's mother had shown great compassion for me, possibly identifying me with her own adopted son's mother.

I recall feeling very uneasy around the guys. I was aware of the fact that I had a "bad" reputation to live down and I thought the best way to do it was to ignore them. Mother said she didn't want me to date for at least six months and I cooperated because I really had no desire to do otherwise. I was still wearing my heart on my sleeve and very much in love with my child's father. I'm not sure to this day that I've gotten over him, but that's what they say about "first love".

Midway through my Junior year, I became active at the "Wishing Well" — a dance that drew people from all over the county. I felt more comfortable around those who were not aware of what had taken place the previous summer. I could be myself. If I met some-one there and was asked for a date, I was more confident that I was being asked for myself rather than for what they might "get".

As the parties at school began to pick up, the tension and friction in our crowd began to increase. Len had started dating a close friend of mine which made for an uneasy relationship all around. She had commented that it was difficult for her to even look at me knowing I had had his child. I'm sure it was a natural feeling for her to have. They continued their relationship and subsequently married.

Some of the guys I dated treated me with perfect respect, while others were sure they were going to score the first time around. I made it quite clear to them that I was not interested in a wrestling match, that they could take me home and that I did not care to date them again. I imagine a few egos were shattered. I was determined to prove that I was not "easy" and that the only reason I had "given in" to Len was because I loved him and, in my mind, that made the difference.

It was around this same time that I received a letter from the court telling me that the finalization of the adoption was about to take place. It went on to state that, because I was a minor, it was not necessary for me to be present. I can remember thinking, "If I could just get there, I could see what the adoptive parents look like". I thought and thought, but was unable to figure out how I could manage it. I would have had to cut school and did not want to chance getting into any more trouble, so I dropped the idea.

In February of my Senior year, I started dating my husband-to-be. All the deep strong feelings I had had for Len were now transferred to my new love. He lived only a block from me and was a year behind my class. Though he knew the whole situation, he treated me with respect. That was the main thing that attracted me to him. Most of our dates were group type — basketball games, pizza parties, etc. I had stopped running with my crowd and started going with his. They were a mischievious bunch, but I enjoyed being with them. They would think nothing of cutting school and going to the shore for the day. (This is no big deal now, but it was then!) In school they were always clowning around. One time a guy put a tack on a girls' chair. She sat down, let out a scream, and they all pointed to another guy who was totally innocent.

I was so wrapped up in school activities that thoughts of my daughter did not emerge until her first birthday. I bought a birthday card, signed it "Mother" and sent it to the pastor of the church I had attended while in the private shelter home. I asked that he be kind enough to forward it. That night I cried and prayed that some day, some way, I would find my child. I relived each birthday in pain and prayer. I could not comprehend that a great and loving God would allow me to go through this whole life and never know the child I had given birth to.

At this point I would like to share with you a letter my mother wrote me when I asked her to express some of the feelings she had at that time. It follows verbatim:

Dearest Sandra:

I am firmly convinced the good Lord wipes unpleasant things out of our minds and gives us that uncanny facility of forgetting things we don't want to remember. What can I tell you? I can only say the initial shock was one of utter disbelief for my sweet little 14 year old daughter. The natural inclination was to turn to our minister for advice. And if my memory serves me correctly, he handled everything from then on. Apparently he must have known someone in the local area who knew the adoptive parents and also the people you stayed with. He also contacted Len's family — I don't ever remember talking with them about it.

As to abortion — the thought never entered my mind. I must confess that it was not only because of principle (I wish I could say it was – I'm certain that had a lot to do with it because of my religious upbringing) but also I had had the unfortunate experience of seeing a roommate of mine almost bleed to death from an illegal abortion. It was just horrible.

I'm sure you know by now, Sandra, that I strongly am of the opinion that everything happens for a reason and I'm sure I felt at that time someone needed that little girl. However, I'm sure, too, that the thought went through my mind – "Where did I fail?" You must know now, being a mother yourself, that I always wanted to do for you kids what I thought was best for you. And then when something like that happens, a mother just can't help blaming herself and wondering what she could have done differently.

But, and I know I'm repeating myself, God has that way of helping us to come thru – you know, He keeps telling us to pray about everything and not to worry about anything. Please be assured, dear one, I am praying so fervently for you – something good is going to happen to you – I know!!

Love,
Mother

Little did I realize how prophetic those last words were. Can you see why I call her a jewel? Her faith in God sustained her through the trauma and I had her total support from the very beginning. While at the time, I did not fully appreciate it, I'm so grateful that I've since had the opportunity to say "Thanks, Mom! Thanks for everything!" I only wish that all young girls who find themselves in a similar circumstance, could have that kind of support. It means so much. That same support has continued throughout the years. She has never failed to be available when I needed her. Several times over the years I'd ask her if she thought my daughter would ever try to locate me. She'd remark with something like, "I hope so, Sandra, for your sake because I know how much it means to you." When I'd inquire about information, she'd reiterate over and over that she didn't know anything. At the time, I thought she was just holding back, but I came to realize that she really didn't have any information to give me.

Looking for the Way

The desire within me to know my daughter grew stronger with each passing year. Somewhere out there in this big world was a part of me, and unless I could find her, I would be left like a broken chain with a missing link.

The days passed quickly with my involvement in child rearing and the many responsibilities that go along with it. I held a full-time job and was active in community affairs, i.e., Brownie leader, P.T.A. board member, Sunday School teacher, but always in the back of my mind is a daughter. I don't know her name or her whereabouts but I pray often for the day we shall meet.

After ten years of marriage and aimlessness in my life, I began to sense that something was wrong. My marriage was falling apart; my life had no real purpose that I could see. The drudgery of going to work each day and coming home to cooking, laundry, four young children, an unattentive husband, had all begun to take its toll. I had come to the place where I really wondered what life was about and whether it was really worth living. The lack of it seemed to be much more appealing than my present existence.

I was at an all-time low when I began to realize that possibly my problem was spiritual. I had been raised in the church, but had never quite grasped the truths. Soon after I married, I decided that I didn't need the church or God, so I gave up both. I had now reached the end of my rope; I was sinking fast. I found myself in need of that which I thought I had no need of – a higher power – a personal God. Someone who could take control of my messed-up life. As I cried out to Him in my misery, I felt a new sense of living come into my being. I began to exercise faith that had lain dormant for so long. I began to

27

claim some of the promises I was discovering in the scriptures. They seemed to be there as little gold nuggets just waiting to be found and claimed for one's own. I clung to them and began to believe that the one single desire of my heart would be fulfilled — to one day find my daughter. Promises like, "Seek first the kingdom of God and His righteousness and all these things shall be added unto you." (Matthew 6:33). "Commit your way unto the Lord, trust in Him, and *He* will bring it to pass." (Psalms 37:5). And finally, "Pray in faith believing, and it shall be yours." (Matthew 21:22). I was uncertain how long I'd have to wait, but, as I thought back over my childhood, I began to see some analogies. I recalled asking mother for a bicycle. It was during the summer months when my pleading began. She said she would get me one for Christmas. I knew that I could depend on my mother's word. The bike was already mine — she had said so, but I had to wait until Christmas. God has proper timing for all our desires. Sometimes we have to wait, but always His timing is right.

I was beginning to see life from a totally new perspective. No more anger at having a daughter out there somewhere that society said I could never know. Rather a peaceful assurance that the day was coming when I'd see her face to face and tell her of my love and the years I had yearned to know her.

One of the questions so often asked by adoptive parent groups and agency staffs is, "Why, having four lovely children, did you desire to seek out this one?" I can only reply by giving the illustration of the Lord as Shepherd. Though there are ninety-nine sheep in the fold, He is constantly in search of that one.

I didn't know why I had the need, anymore than I understand why the Lord is always in search of His own reconciling them to Himself. The only difference is that we, as His children, have chosen by our very nature to go our own way; whereas in the case of adoption, a mother, because of circumstances, has to surrender her child. She never stops caring. The fact cannot be changed that there is a bond in giving life that cannot be broken. I have received hundreds of letters from birthparents and have yet to hear a birthparent say, "I *never* want to meet my child." Yes, in most cases, there is fear involved — fear that the child has contempt for the parent — a real fear with which the birthparent has to come to grips. Having that fear removed, the birthparent gladly welcomes their child. The story of the Prodigal Son is also a story about the size of a Father's heart, always big enough to welcome His child no matter what the intervening years had wrought. Love, unconditional love, always wins out. Most birthparents have that kind of love. In giving up their child,

28

they had to give so much of themselves.

My heart is open, not only to my daughter, but to her whole adoptive family. I feel as though they are an extension of my own, that I could develop a relationship with them similar to that which I have with other extended family members. I love them because they accepted the responsibility of raising my daughter when I was unable to do so and I am grateful. She was entrusted to their care and they did their job well. All children are entrusted to the care of their parents – God foreordained that. They belong to Him, but He's put them in our care. We are expected to do the best we know how to raise them to adulthood and then set them free to soar on their own course. They are only loaned to us – whether natural or adopted – to love them and train them during the brief years that we have them. As the plaque says which hangs under the pictures of my children – "There are only two lasting bequests we can give our children – One is roots – the other is wings".

It dawned on me recently that Moses may have been the first adoptee (Exodus 2:10). He was a Hebrew child raised by an Egyptian family (a well-to-do family!). That seems to be one of the things birthparents are always told about the placement of their children. His mother hid him in the bushes as there had been an edict handed down to destroy all Hebrew male infants. The daughter of Pharoah came to bathe in the water and found the child and took pity on him. His sister Miriam, who had been told by her mother to keep watch over him, offered to find a nurse for the child – who turned out to be his own mother! How fortunate for her! She could watch her child grow into manhood – something which the rest of us have been denied. Moses, we are told, had the privilege of gaining substantial training in the "wisdom of the Egyptians". His education was undoubtedly a fine one. While little is said about his growth to adulthood, we are told that he felt strongly for his kin. He had a *natural* longing for his family. Are things any different for adoptees today? Thousands of years later, they still long to know their roots, as did Moses. Birthparents, as well, long to know how their children have fared over the years.

29

My Search Begins

My search began in April of 1976. Arriving home from work one bright spring afternoon, I sat down to relax with the local newspaper; something which I seldom found time to do. As I was reading, I caught sight of a reunion story – one P. Partridge of Philadelphia had just recently been reunited with her mother after 32 years. My heart leaped as I began to imagine the possibility of such a meeting with a daughter I had never forgotten. I reached for the phone to call information and as I did, sent a quick prayer heavenward that I might locate this fortunate one who had just found her mother. The operator said the usual, "Can I help you?" and as my heart pounded away, I replied, "Yes, operator, I'm trying to locate a P. Partridge of Philadelphia." Within a few minutes, which seemed endless, she gave me a number. I couldn't believe it! There was actually a listing! Was it the same person? My heart beat faster. As I picked up the phone to dial the number, I prayed again; this time audibly. "Lord, you know the desire of my heart. If this is meant to be, the person on the other end of the phone will somehow enlighten me." "Hello, my name is Sandy. Are you the same person whose reunion was in the paper?" The reply came back – "Yes, I just met my birthmother for the first time." This was the first time that I had heard the term "birthmother" used, but it was not to be the last. "I was wondering if you might be able to help me or give me some advice." I proceeded with my story. When I was through, I had the verification I needed. "Your daughter would be so pleased to know that you are taking the initiative to find her!" I felt ten feet tall. This was the first time since my experience that anyone had said anything even remotely positive to me about my desire – but then – I had never felt the freedom to share it with

31

anyone before. Could this be a built-in guilt complex?

It was that phone conversation which opened the door to my year-long search. As we spoke I felt my spirits being lifted as I talked with the girl on the other end of the phone. Though we had never met, we shared a common bond. She an adoptee and I a birthmother — there was an immediate understanding of the inner drive that caused us to carry on this seemingly illicit conversation. The guilt re- turned. Should I be doing this? Should I leave well-enough alone? Should I be delving into the past? Would I be creating more problems than I'd be solving? But suddenly I was jolted back to reality by remembering that just the hello that I heard on the other end of the phone was the answer I had needed. In the days that followed, I would utter up my feeble prayers. "Lord, I'm forging ahead in this search — I know that you are able to close doors as well as to open them. I pray simply that your will be done."

The joy that filled me that evening is hard to put into words. It was the first time in 22 years that I had actually verbalized my feelings to another human being — a stranger at that — and yet a stranger that truly understood! A feeling of peace came over me and as I put my head on the pillow that evening, I humbly said, "Thank you, Lord."

I had to wait three weeks before the first meeting of the Adoption Forum. Penny, to whom I had spoken on the phone, was one of the two founders of the group. She had stressed how important it would be for me to attend the meetings in order to have the support of others and to eventually be able to give it. I was scared! I didn't know what to expect, but I was driven by my strong desire to find my daughter. On May 20, 1976, I attended the first of many such meetings. I sat in a small living room and listened while adoptees shared their frustrations, feelings, and thoughts. As they went around the room introducing themselves, one woman said "My name is Barbara and I am a birthmother". A birthmother! Another birth- mother just like me! She also wanted to know her daughter. How fantastic! Someone I could relate to! Why it is that we think we're are the only person in the world with a given feeling about a partic- ular experience. Why hadn't I realized that there must be thousands of others like myself feeling this pain of separation from flesh and blood? Why did I think I was so unique? Possibly because I was never able to share this dark secret with anyone before — because of the fear of condemnation — for fear of reprisal — for fear of rejection? Now I could openly say "My name is Sandy and I am a birthmother." Sympathetic eyes looked and listened as I told my story. As it poured forth I felt a sense of relief. Another weight had been lifted from my shoulders.

Total freedom was becoming mine. I was gaining acceptance about the one remaining secret in my life and it felt good. Surely I had been led to this place, not only to take from it, but to give to it. That has been my pleasure in the last three years — to reach out and help other birthparents who are experiencing the same pain that I had. I had come a long way — from darkness into light as I began to bare my soul to those who had traveled the same path.

Due to another commitment, I was unable to attend the June meeting, but I desperately wanted to keep in touch so I contacted one of the adoptees who lived close by in New Jersey. I called Liz and we began a friendship which led us both to our "impossible dream" — each of us having an active part in the other's search and reunion.

During our first phone conversation, we made arrangements to go to the County Court House. A week or so before we went, I called and spoke to the Clerk of the Orphans' Court (the court that handles adoptions) and told him I was interested in having my married name and new address attached to the adoption record. He stated that he had never had such a request and he would have to discuss the matter with the judge. I had no further contact with him until one day in July when we appeared in his office to make the same request.

We had hoped to speak directly with the judge, but unfortunately he was on vacation. The same clerk I had spoken to on the phone informed me that he had discussed my proposal with the judge and that his reply was, "Who does she think she is to come back here after 20 years and want to find her daughter. If she didn't want her then, why should she bother now!" Hurt and anger welled up inside me as I heard those harsh, condemning words and fought to hold back the tears. Hurt to think that any intelligent person could make such a ridiculous statement and anger that they make statements about something which they apparently know so little. Anger as I realized the immensity of the problem and that I was at this particular judge's mercy. Angry enough now to decide that I was going to throw myself into the whole adoption issue and work towards making the adoption process more humane! I left the courthouse that day determined to see change take place and I was going to have a part in it.

As we drove out of town, I suggested to Liz that we drive to the next town and visit the private shelter home where I had spent the last few months of my pregnancy. The Brysons were warm people whom I had come to love in the short time I spent with them. They lived in a large Tudor style home in a lovely tree-lined section of town. As we drove onto their street, my mind was flooded with memories of so many years before. I became suddenly aware of the beauty of the area and recollected my complete indifference to it as a teenager. I had been so wrapped up in myself that I failed to see the beauty that was all around me. As we walked up the ivy-strewn path, approximately 250 feet, I thought about how little I had appreciated this home, its surroundings, and its occupants.

A knock on the back door brought the "lady" of the home. She was a lady in the truest sense of the word — a well-bred woman. Her sweet, beautiful smile immediately reminded me that for a short time she had been a substitute mother — one whom I had grown to love. I regretted that I had not kept in touch with her. I had written only twice in the 22 years of my absence. Nevertheless, she greeted me with love and affection. We were ushered into the formal living room and given some iced tea to quench our thirst. We spoke about light things until I was unable to contain myself any longer and blurted out, "Mrs. Bryson, I would like to find my daughter. Would you be able to give me any information or do you know where she was placed?" I could feel kindness and understanding in her voice as she replied that she didn't know anything concerning the whereabouts of my daughter. She did know, however, that Dr. Knight, the minister of her Presbyterian Church, had been the intermediary in the case. "Why don't you contact him?" She then told me that he had been transferred some years ago to New York and gave me an address where I could reach him. I was thrilled just to have that much information to go on. I had always thought that he had played an active part, but was never quite sure of his actual involvement. Now I knew for sure. She cautioned me to be careful and warned of the possible consequences, This was a typical reaction which I had come to accept from those outside the adoption triad. I thanked her for her hospitality and told her I would keep in touch with her to let her know the outcome.

As Liz and I left the area, we floated back to Jersey, pleased with what we had learned. One door had been closed, but another had just opened.

Within the next few months, I wrote several letters. I wanted to get and to give as much information as I could. I wrote to the hospital where my daughter was born to see if I could get a certificate of birth. They sent me back a form which stated "I hereby certify according to our records, Baby Musser was born to Mr. and Mrs.

Musser on 7/18/54." This was incorrect as Mr. Musser was not the father nor was I a Mrs. I wrote back and told them of the incorrect information, but never received a reply or correction. I then wrote to the doctor who had delivered my child to see if I could get a copy of my medical file in hopes of obtaining a lead. They wrote that Dr. Corbett had since passed away and that because of the length of time which had lapsed, they no longer had my records.

Following that I wrote to the Department of Public Welfare in Harrisburg to express my interest in being available to my daughter should she ever search for me. They wrote a beautiful letter assuring me that they would keep the information on file and make it available to her should she ever inquire as to my whereabouts. As you can see, I was leaving few stones unturned.

Summer was over. Fall had arrived. I received an inquiry from a lawyer in Vineland asking if I would be willing to testify in a case which he was handling concerning adoption. Four adoptees were seeking to have their records opened by petitioning the court. The hearing was scheduled for late September in Atlantic City. I wrote back to Mr. Shapiro stating my willingness to testify, but that I was due for an operation during that time. In lieu of my presence, I wrote up a detailed description of my feelings and submitted the letter to him to be used as he saw fit. As it turned out, the trial was not held until the latter part of October and I was able to testify. As a result of that case, Judge Gruccio determined that the psychological "need to know" may constitute sufficient cause to open the records. This decision was handed down with several stipulations attached. Many adoptees were disappointed – others felt that it was a step in the right direction. However, we've still got a long way to go before *adult* adoptees are treated as adults and not as eternal children.

Finally on November 6, I sat down and wrote a letter to Rev. Knight. It had taken me three months to get around to it. It had been that long since my visit to Mrs. Bryson. Now I felt ready to pursue this avenue. My letter to the pastor follows:

Dear Rev. Knight:

I am writing this letter to you prayerfully and with high hopes that you will be willing to assist me.

My name is Sandra Musser, and if you recall, I gave my child up for adoption back in 1954. I was staying with the Bryson's at the time. It is my understanding, from the searching I've already done, that you were or are the one that arranged the adoption and knew the family.

My reason for writing is simply this — I have never forgotten my daughter. I realize that I cannot contact her. My intent and purpose for writing this letter is to ask if you would notify the parents of my interest in her and that I am very anxious to be located if she should be wondering about me. Let me make it clear that I do not want to cause anyone any problems, but that I do long to meet and know her if she should desire same.

I am enclosing much "leg" work already done in my endeavor and feel you are my last resort. If nothing else, I would appreciate your response expressing your feelings, etc. Since my daughter is now an adult at 22, I feel that no one can be hurt by our meeting.

As you can see by the enclosed papers, I am not alone in this turmoil. You hold the key to calming the many inner feelings that this mother has had in giving up her child. It's with a pleading heart that I make this request.

As a born-again Christian, I have sought the Lord's will in this and have felt led to move ahead in the present direction. My prayer now is that you will give my request thought and consideration.

I will be anxiously awaiting your reply.

Most sincerely,
Sandy Musser

I waited three weeks and when I did not hear from him, I wrote again. This time I stated that whether or not he agreed with my request, he at least owed me the courtesy of a reply. His answer came shortly thereafter:

Dear Sandy:

Please forgive my delay in answering your letter. I have been prompted by your recent letter to get back to you — I hope you will forgive me for I know how urgent this matter is to your heart.

My delay in answering has been somewhat dictated by a good deal of thought and prayer on my part as to what the Lord's will will be in this matter.

I find myself however, now in agreement with you that the whole question really revolves around your daughter herself and I have every faith that your primary concern is for her happiness and her continued stability and enjoyment of life. Therefore, I have taken steps to reach her to determine if she would be interested in being reunited with her

36

natural mother. I know from your correspondence that you will also agree with me that the feelings of the family who have raised her over the years also must be considered. However, if there is no objection from either side, you may be sure that I will do everything I can to see that a reunion takes place and as soon as I have any pertinent information on the questions I raised in this letter, I will be in touch with you at once.

Sincerely,

I was flying high after that letter: The next six weeks were probably the longest I can remember as I awaited word as to what my daughter's response would be.

January 19 I went to Penn State to speak to a group of adoptive parents. This was my second speaking engagement. My feet were getting wet and I enjoyed the opportunity to be able to exchange views and ideas with adoptive parents. It was the beginning of many opportunities to follow.

I arrived home the evening of the 20th, weary from the trip, to find a letter from Rev. Knight. My heart pounded as I tore it open and read the following lines:

I have been in touch with your daughter, as well as with her adopted family, and their present position in regard to your proposition is that they are not prepared to cooperate at this time. It is a new idea to them. They took some time to reflect upon it. They seriously sought the guidance of God's will for their lives in this matter and came to the conclusion that the time was not right.

Your daughter is now, as you know, a mature woman and is also married. Her husband, at the moment, would be most opposed to any such reunion. Your daughter is also reluctant because she feels that it would introduce a whole new psychological element of stress which she is not prepared, at this time, to handle.

Everyone is most sympathetic with your prospective and understands your desires completely, but they are all agreed that life has moved along in a fairly steady path. It has not been without its times of difficulties, and the impression that I get is that they are now in a smooth and open road and would rather enjoy that for a while before introducing any new possibility of stress.

Your daughter is fine and is a person highly regarded and respected by everyone. She has enjoyed the family with whom she has grown up and is very close to both of her adopted parents. She also has two

37

brothers who are younger than herself.

They would wish me to assure you that should their minds change or should they feel that the Lord has led them to another conclusion, that they will be in touch with me. I could not find out from them what kind of time they had in mind, or did I feel it was appropriate for me to press the issue any further. So I shall plan to keep this correspondence, and should they be in touch with me about it, you may be sure that I will write you at once.

Please be assured that you're in my prayers.

Warmest regards,

My eyes, by this time, were filled to overflowing! My dreams were shattered! The door had closed.

It's difficult to express the feelings I had at that moment. Deep disappointment, sadness, rejection, all welled up inside me. When I began my search, I remember thinking that I had to face up to the possibility that my daughter might not be willing to meet me. It was a fear that I knew I had to deal with. I thought I had. At one of the meetings, I had even shared how I was facing up to the possibility of rejection. Now the test had come. Was I going to pass it? I wasn't sure.

A few days later I sat down and wrote another letter to Rev. Knight. I thanked him for his time and cooperation. "I am very grateful to you for your help and am confident that time will be the victor". I then asked him for his assurance that all correspondence would be kept and/or turned over upon his demise. I ended by stating that, "I know that the Lord is soverign and His timing is perfect. Knowing that he is in full control of the situation certainly takes some of the sharp edge off my disappointment."

His final letter to me arrived three weeks later, assuring me that the correspondence would be kept in a safe place so as to be available always to the secretary should anything happen to him. He closed his letter by saying, "I have been given assurance that should these decisions change in any way that they will write me and request an opportunity to be in touch with you. I told them of your own commitment to the Lord and of your steadfast and undying interest in the future of your daughter no matter what may come".

Again the waiting began. The speaking engagements were picking up. More and more adoptive parents' groups wanted to hear a "real" birthmother. I was baring my soul each time I said, "My name is Sandy and I am a birthmother". Each time I did, it became easier and healing was taking place. I would continue with, "I gave up a child for adoption when I was 15 years old, but I have never forgotten her" — and so it went. Adoptive parents were also beginning to open up and share their feelings — feelings of "losing their children" to the birthparent. Many of them stated quite vehemently that they were against open records — it is a threat to their relationship with their adopted child.

Interestingly I have noted that this most often comes from the older generation of adoptive parents. The younger ones seem much more receptive to the new ideas and thoughts being introduced regarding innovative adoption procedures.

There are so many facets to the adoption issue — an important aspect is the plight of the adoptive parent. In attempting to understand their feelings, I realized that I would need to put myself in their place. I was not sure I was going to be able to do that, but I needed to try for the sake of fairness, understanding, and compassion. Being an extremely fertile individual, I was now going to have to comprehend the feelings surrounding infertility. The heartache of wanting a child so desperately, of trying for years, of having all the tests — these things I needed to understand.

I also needed to realize that when finally being able to adopt a child, that child becomes their very own and quite naturally, they do not want anyone to infer anything different. Could this be one of the reasons for the adoptive parents' opposition to open records? Open records meaning that a person upon reaching majority age may obtain the information on their original certificate (regardless of their reasons for doing so). Do they feel threatened that their now grown children will transfer their love or loyalty to the newfound parent? When thinking it through logically, this just doesn't happen, any more than it does when one marries. Yes, there is a new relationship involved, but it does not change the relationship with one's parents. If anything it may tend to enhance it. Nor does the knowledge of one's roots change the love that is felt for the people who raised you — your parents! As a mother of four teenagers, I have come to realize that once they have reached maturity, I have no right to "hang on" to them. I would not want to if I could. Each has to use their own wings to search out their own impossible dream — whatever that dream may be.

In the case of many adoptees, that impossible dream is knowing their roots. Each of us as individuals have the constitutional right to our own pursuit of happiness — except for the adoptee. Roadblocks have been put up to protect them from the "big, dark secret" which surrounds their birth. Who is being protected from what? As adults, adoptees must face all the other realities of life that come to each of us at one time or another. That's part of life. Do we really believe that they are unable to handle the facts which surround their birth — no matter what they may be. Facts are always easier to deal with than the unknown. With the unknown comes fear, but when the unknown factor is removed, fear is gone. Reality can be dealt with.

If a close relationship has been developed, then we can allow those loved ones to use their wings with confidence. In the case of the adoptee, the adoptive parent may want to offer whatever assistance they can in helping them obtain their sought-after roots. In so doing they will be helping to shed light which will lead them to their much needed truth.

Soon after receiving the letter from the Pastor, I was invited to do a program for Channel 10 called "Update" with Herb Clark, two adoptees, and a social worker. After explaining my story and bringing the facts up to date, Herb Clark asked me what my feelings were now that I had been "rejected". I responded with "I have a lot of faith, and still believe the day is coming when we are going to meet." Little did I know then that our reunion was only a few short months away. Much sooner than I had expected, but a reminder to me that "... with God, all things are possible" (Matthew 19:26).

For the next month and a half, I kept wondering if I had left anything undone. I began to read and reread all the correspondence I had since my search began. As I methodically did this, a thought suddenly occurred to me. While I was reading over the letters from the Pastor, I began to wonder if he had been in direct contact with my daughter or if the information he had relayed to me had come through the adoptive parents. As I pondered this possibility, I thought about what I could do to determine if this was true. The Easter holiday was approaching and being a school secretary, I would have a week off — time enough to take a trip to New York to pay a personal visit to my penpal.

In reading through the ALMA (Adoptees Liberty Movement Association) newsletter, I noticed that there would be a meeting of their adoption group during the same period. Now I could kill two birds with one stone. On April 10, 1977, I sat in a church in New York with approximately 150 adoptees and birthparents in attendance. The panel discussion that day was adoptees who had searched for and found their birthparents. As they described their feelings, a variation of emotions emerged, each story different, each story special.

Following the meeting, it was announced that there would be

search workshops for anyone who needed assistance. They stressed the fact that adoptees must be over the age of 18, and that the birthparents' child must also be over the age of 18. I followed the crowd of searchers into a small room where we waited in turn for our name to be called. We had previously filled out a form giving as much information as we knew to aid those who would be assisting us. I spent no more than seven or eight minutes with a gentleman who gave me a quick suggestion and said if it didn't work to return and we'd try another avenue. I left that day very excited about the chance that I might be on the threshhold of my lifelong dream.

It was early evening as I left that old church and I knew that there was no possible way that I was going to be able to get to see my pastor-friend. He was about 60 miles away. However, while chatting after the meeting, a woman mentioned that she lived in his vicinity. She invited me to come up during the week and volunteered to drive me to his church and/or residence. What an opportunity!

I came home that evening weary, but ecstatic. My spirits had been lifted being in the presence of those of kindred minds. They understood my need and drive and I understood theirs. We were all traveling the same course – the course that would lead us to our impossible dream; the course that up until now had been blocked off.

The following day I sat down and wrote the letter that would eventually gain me access to my daughter's name, and again the waiting began. I made plans to go back up to New York the following Saturday in order to talk with Rev. Knight. The adoptee I had met at the ALMA meeting would meet me at the train and transport me to the church. Arriving in New York about lunchtime, we went to a lovely restaurant where we shared our intimate stories. She, an adoptee of 52, was just beginning to search having waited until her adoptive parents died so as not to hurt them. This is so often true. The adoptee waits until their adoptive parents are deceased before beginning an active search. Is this a guilt-trip that has been laid on them by their parents – is it an innate feeling they have or are given since they are told so often how appreciative they should be? Whatever the reason, whatever the cause, many adoptees do feel guilty about the whole idea of searching and how to go about telling their adoptive parents. One of the first questions asked by an adoptee coming into the Adoption Forum group for the first time is, "How do I go about telling my adoptive parents that I want to search? I know they won't understand, I know they'll be hurt – they'll think they've failed me in some way and they haven't – how can I tell them that it's something I *have* to do?"

41

Hope and I finished up our delicious lunch and were on our way
—the butterflies in my stomach wasted no time in fluttering around
and upsetting my equilibrium. I was about to meet the one person
who could put me in touch with my daughter – the one who knew
the family, who had been so closely involved 22 years hence. It was
this man to whom I sent my daughter's birthday cards the first five
years of her life and asked that they be forwarded, never knowing if
they were. As we drove along the winding streets in Barley, New
York, I thought of the things I wanted to convey. Anxious, too, for
the pastor to meet me and observe that I was not an irrational person
or out to cause any problems. I was no longer that 15 year old girl
"in trouble". I was now a grown, mature woman, with feelings of
concern for a child I had never forgotten. I was extremely apprehen-
sive, considering the fact that I was dropping in on him "cold" –
intentionally – not wanting to give him time to "get his story
together."

We finally arrived at the church, which had the appearance of a
cathedral; it was so big and beautiful – all stone – standing tall and
proud against the backdrop of a blue sky, and bushy green trees with
their brown branches stretching upwards toward their Creator. As we
drove up the massive driveway, we were indecisive as to which door
we should enter. Glancing to our left we saw what we assumed was
the parsonage. Our inclination was correct. The housekeeper answered
the door, informed us that the pastor was next door at the church
and told us which door to use to get to his office. As we climbed the
stairs leading to the pastor's study, we were met by a secretary who
was just on her way out to lunch. I told her my name, stated that I
had known Pastor Knight when he was in Pennsylvania, and hoped to
chat with him briefly while I was in town. She went away and came
back in a few minutes and asked that we please have a seat; he would
be right with us.

He entered the room where we were sitting and warmly greeted
me by name. I was struck by the fact that his appearance had not
changed much over the years. After a quick introduction of my
friend, we were escorted into his office. We exchanged small talk and
the butterflies continued their flight. After about ten minutes I was
able to get down to business, down to the purpose of my visit. Had
he spoken directly to my daughter? What I had suspected was true.
No, he had not. The information he had relayed to me through his
letter was what he had received via the adoptive parents. Anger at
once welled up within me though I contained it. My mind was
thinking, "Who did they think they were to make a decision for a 23

year old mature adult? How did they arrive at their decision?" The pastor went on to express his feeling that the adoptive parents' opinion concerning reunion is important. I agreed, but not to the point where they make a decision which totally excludes the adoptees' choice in the matter. Would he please make a personal contact with her and then get back to me? He promised he would while not giving me any time period. However, I felt relieved knowing that he had not spoken to her personally and also his willingness to do so.

As we walked out into the April sunlight, with the birds singing, the warm breezes blowing, I knew it had been a worthwhile trip. My daughter had not rejected me, though her parents had.

Hope drove me back to the train station and I was on my way back to Jersey to await the outcome of whatever was to be. I was hopeful that something was going to break soon.

It did. Within four days of that trip, I received my daughter's name in the mail in response to the letter I had written ten days previously. I've not had correspondence with the pastor to this day, but I imagine he's been in touch with the adoptive family and knows the outcome of this story.

The name arrived on a Thursday. For the next three days I floated around with a feeling of intoxication as I repeated her name over and over. It was music to my ears. That person "out there somewhere" in that big wide world now had a name. I no longer had to speak about her in an abstract kind of way. She actually existed — she was real — she had a name.

By Sunday night I was beginning to come back to earth and plan my strategy for the next day. I called my sister in Havertown and asked her to check the name in the phone book. She did. There was only one listing and I knew with certainty it was the adoptive parents. I then called my friend Liz, and made plans for the next day to go back to the County Court House and delve into the marriage licenses. I would need to find out her married name in order to pursue the course I was now on, and complete my search.

The following day Liz and I met my sister Terry at my other sister's home. From there I called the school district to determine what high school my daughter had attended. I was so anxious to see a picture of her. After getting that information we were on our way. Expectancy and anticipation were thick in the air. I was about to see her face for the first time — in a high school yearbook! We entered the main office and inquired about the possibility of looking at some old yearbooks. The woman told us they were kept in the library and directed us down a nearby corridor. We decided that since Terry was

43

the youngest, she should be the one to inquire on the premise of looking up an old classmate. The librarian showed us where they were and told us to help ourselves. We were expecting all kinds of static and it was so easy! I am normally a rather calm, easy-going person, but by this time my whole body was shaking. As we sat down at a table, book in hand, I began flipping through the Ns. My eyes were moving slowly over each picture while, at the same time, I was noting names. And then – there she was! My daughter's face. I was seeing my daughter's face for the first time in 23 years in a high school yearbook. I wanted to laugh, cry, sing, jump! I wanted to tear the picture out of the book and run as fast as I could. Instantly I saw likenesses of her father. She has his eyes and smile. Her hair was long and brown, parted in the middle. As I feasted my eyes upon the photograph, all the intervening years I had missed welled up within me. Liz and Terry were making comments, but they were not registering in my mind. I had shut the two of them out as I stared at my daughter. This moment was wholly mine. I made it so! It was as though there were no one else in the room – just Cindy and I – together at last.

Once I gained my composure, we decided to go to the court house. As we approached the tall building, my mind returned to the nine months before and the angry feelings that the judge's statements had aroused within me. Immediately we went to the information desk and inquired as to where the marriage records were kept. We were directed down a long hallway and entered a room which was lined on all sides with huge books. Not knowing where or how to begin, we asked one of the attendants for help. He explained that the books had listings of names of marriages which had taken place in any given year. First you would locate the year and then look alphabetically for the name you wanted to find. Upon finding it, directly across would be the name of the person they married. For four dollars we could get a copy of the marriage certificate or we could look at it for nothing and take whatever information we wanted from it – since marriage records are open to the public. We did the latter which helped to verify the fact that it was who we were looking for. Another milestone had been reached. I now know her married name. We began guessing what nationality it was. Like her adoptive name, it was not a common one.

"Okay, girls, what now?" My thoughts were becoming blurred with all the happenings of the one day – finding her parents name and address, seeing her picture for the first time, and now knowing her married name! Everything was happening so fast! Liz said, "Back to the phone book!" We found a phone booth and quickly found the name we were looking for. There were only two listings. They were both in the same town and, as it turned out, only one block apart. God seemed to be opening doors quicker than I could walk through them. Step by step things were falling into place. The confrontation was close at hand. Was I prepared for it?

"Well, let's just ride by the place and then we can decide what to do". We got out the old map, found the location and headed out of town. Soon we found ourselves on the street we were looking for and excitement for all of us was running high. Liz and Terry were like a couple of high school kids, chatting and giggling and I was more solemn, wondering just what it was that was about to happen. That's it over there — that's the house. It looks like it might be a duplex. Okay, pull down the street a little way so we can decide what to do." Liz suggested, "What if Terry and I knock on the door and tell whoever answers that we're in the area looking for an apartment — at least that way we can get a look and see if it's her." "Good idea." Terry responded.

At this point my body was actually trembling as the two of them left the car and approached the house. I was some 50 feet away, so could not see clearly as the door opened and someone appeared. Liz and Terry carried on a conversation that lasted seven to eight minutes. Were they talking to my daughter? The suspense was unbearable! Returning to the car, Liz said "Congratulations — you are the grandmother of two!" I said "you're kidding!" She went on to say "Her father-in-law owns this duplex they are living in. The girl we spoke to said that the couple who live upstairs are the son and daughter-in-law of the owner who lives around the corner." It all made sense. According to the phone book, the father-in-law did live on the next street over.

We decided to pay a visit to the in-laws under the same pretense — finding an apartment in the area. This time I decided to be the door-knocker along with Liz while Terry remained in the car. A nice-looking gentleman appeared at the door and we said, "We understand that you own the duplex around the corner and were wondering if one of the apartments might be available." He laughed as he said "Oh, no, I don't own that building — one of the neighbors down the street does!" We chatted for a few minutes about the possibility of finding work in the area due to the industry, etc. We found him to be very pleasant and congenial. My daughter's father-in-law! This was now the closest I'd been to anyone who knew her personally. I wanted to say, "Tell me about your daughter-in-law. What is she like? Do you have a good relationship with her?" These thoughts were going through my mind as we discussed incidentals — he, of course, not realizing who I was and me too fearful to tell him, though I desperately wanted to. He was so friendly and warm that I thought he might even respond with, "Great, I'll call her up and tell her you're here!"

We went back to the apartment to get an answer as to why things weren't matching up. Again Liz and Terry went to the door and again spoke to the same girl. "Was Cindy ＿＿＿＿＿＿ the girl who lived upstairs?" "Oh, no," came the reply, "She moved a few months ago." Now we understood. The new tenants were the relatives of the owner. They thanked the girl and we left. Liz had to get back to Jersey in time to meet her children from school and so we were unable to do anything more that day.

The following day Terry and I drove back to the local post office and for the cost of one dollar obtained a change of address under the Freedom of Information Act.

Dispelling the Shadows

April 26, 1977, one week after receiving her name, I sat down and wrote the following letter to my daughter:

Dear Cindy:

For so many years I've longed to say those words — the precious name of a daughter I had to give up because I was too young to care for her.

Words are insufficient in trying to express the feelings that are in my heart for you. I've prayed for this day to come — the day I'd know who you are and where you are. The Lord has answered the very longings of my heart. Just to know your name and that you've happily married gives me a sense of joy.

It is my sincere desire to meet with you, if only briefly. I do not wish to interfere in your life or cause you any problems, but just to see you and fill in all the missing years. I understand you had wonderful parents and I am so grateful to them.

I expect to be in Wilmington on the 14th of May and wondered if we could get together on that day. I will await your reply. Also I'd love you to send a picture of yourself.

> Longing to know you —
> Sandy
> (your "birth" mother and friend)

I could have picked up the telephone. I had called information to see if there was a listing. There was. I took what I considered to be the easier method of contact. In retrospect I was fearful of being rejected outright in a phone conversation. I tried to keep my letter brief and to the point. To be sure she received it, I sent it by registered mail.

Four days later the card came back signed by her husband. At first I was angry. What if her husband had opened my letter, was completely opposed to the idea of a reunion and never told her about receiving it? How would I be sure she even read my letter?

My questions were answered about a week later. I received a letter from her adoptive mother which was both loving and kind. She wrote:

Dear Sandy:

Although we have never met, we have played a role in each other's lives. Last January, Rev. Knight wrote to tell us of your letter to him. We made a considered judgement then, that the time was not right for Cindy to meet you. There is no need to go into our rationale for we live in a constant changing world. However, I will mention that I had discussed the "Right to Know" concept with her and knew of her feelings.

I can readily appreciate your desire and your determination to seek her out. And right now, you must be anxiously awaiting some word from her. She did try to call you the night she received your letter. Her mood had somewhat shifted since the first shock and she does intend to write to you. Her initial reaction was one of an invasion of her privacy and the fact that she should have a choice to "know" before the fact. I am writing this note to urge you to be patient. She does intend to write and I have every confidence that as she lives with the idea for a while that she will grant your request. I can only caution you again to be patient. You have lived with this hope for years; do not prejudice the outcome by not giving her adequate time to adjust.

We have no idea how you were able to locate her, but I know that where there is a will, there is a way. Cindy and I have discussed your letter and she has my encouragement to respond. However, her father has some reservations about the idea and this is one of the reasons that she must be given time to collect all of her thoughts and decide how to proceed. She is going on vacation May 13 and she has told me she intends to write you before she leaves.

I can assure you – she's worth waiting for.

In Friendship,

As I read her letter through several times, many emotions began to emerge. The following day I responded:

Dear Mrs. Nanreit:

I cannot tell you how pleased I was to receive your note. I was able to determine from it that you are a compassionate and understanding person and I'm extremely grateful to the Lord that he chose you to raise and nurture the child I gave birth to. There are so many things I'd like to share with you and I don't know whether I'm going to be able to convey my feelings on paper or not, but I'm going to try.

As you probably know, I was 15 years old at the time I gave birth. While I have never forgotten her and while many a night I cried and prayed that some day we'd meet, I still believed that I had done the best thing by her and for her. After receiving your letter, I am more sure of that fact than ever before. I realize that I cannot be a mother — you have already fulfilled the role so very well. My only desire is to have a chance to meet her and if possible, to be a friend. As stated by you, that will have to be her decision and if and when she is ready. I have done all I can do by taking the initiative and now it's in her hands. Thank you for your words of encouragement — they were both helpful and appreciated.

Several times over the years I'd ask mother if she thought my daughter would try to locate me. She'd just comment with, "I don't know Sandra, but I hope for your sake because I know how much it would mean to you." She was right — and you were right — I have lived with this hope for years. People have asked why I would want to search for a daughter I gave up when I have four other children. My only response is to use the allegory of the Lord while having 99 in the fold is always in search of that one. I don't know why He seeks out one anymore than I know why I have the need. I don't mean to infer that she is "lost", but only to use the illustration as far as feelings are concerned. My feelings are real and since feelings are neither right nor wrong, I have learned to accept them.

Please feel free to write me again. It would be a privilege for me to meet you. Maybe we can get together sometime soon, at your convenience and willingness. Thank you again for your kind and thoughtful note. It meant a lot to me. I shall certainly use all my patience as I await Cindy's reply.

Most sincerely,
Sandy

My patience ran out on May 26, 1977, one month from the date I had written my first letter. My persistent streak came through as I wrote:

Dear Cindy:

It's been a month now since I first wrote you. I had hoped you would grant me a reply. Each day I've awaited some word from you. I guess I'm more ready to deal with a rejection than hearing nothing and not knowing what you feel.

However, since I did make the initial contact and since it is not my desire to pester you, I won't write again unless I hear from you. I do want you to know that I've never forgotten you and never will — regardless of the outcome.

I'll be here whenever you feel you're ready. Again — I'm so thankful you had a happy home and I'll continue to pray that only good things come your way.

> With Much Love,
> Sandy

From the beginning of my search I had kept all correspondence relating to it. At the bottom of the above letter, there is now a notation that says "Cindy called — 5/28/77 — PTL" (Praise the Lord!).

That evening at 8:45 p.m. I answered the telephone and heard someone say, "Is Sandy there?" The voice was unfamiliar and I replied, "This is Sandy". The next thing I heard was, "Hi, this is Cindy." My mind literally swirled as I very feebly said, "Cindy?" and then very softly (as if the sound of my voice would make her fade away), "Hi, Cindy." I felt as though I were in a dream. I kept thinking to myself, "Is this really happening? Is it possible? Is this my daughter on the other end of the phone?" I was fearful that any minute I would wake up and realize that it was just a dream. I recall wanting to say "just the right thing" (whatever that is!). Thoughts continued to swirl. "Does she like the sound of my voice? Are there questions I shouldn't ask?" She continued the conversation by first apologizing for taking so long to respond to my letter and explained that her feelings were very mixed and that her father was opposed to any contact, which was causing a problem for her. I suggested that possibly it was because she is his only daughter and that he was acting in a protective manner.

50

She then informed me that her parents had never told her that I had been in touch with Rev. Knight. She said she guessed they were trying to protect her as she had been having some marital difficulties at that time. She also said she was surprised because her mother had never kept anything from her before and had always been very open about the "right to know". She then proceeded to tell me that back in the fall of 1976, she had gone to the County Court House to see if she could get information about her background. She was told that the records were closed and that she would need a court order showing "good cause" to have them opened. She knew that would involve retaining a lawyer and probably cost a lot of money, so she set the idea aside having no alternative. I informed her that I had been to the courthouse in July of 1976 requesting that my name and address be put into the records in case she would ever want to locate me. Again — interference from "outsiders" made an earlier reunion impossible!

Many times during our half-hour conversation I felt like an observer — as though I were actually watching what was taking place. We discussed the circumstances of her birth — the fact that we were both young. She was extremely interested in her nationality; most people thought she was Italian. I told her that I have a German background and her father was Irish. We talked about our families. She was raised with two younger brothers — one an adoptee and the other natural.

We ended our conversation by agreeing to write and exchange pictures. As I hung up the phone, I bowed my head in prayer and thanked God for that highlight in my life. I then floated around the room and if anyone had seen me, they would surely have thought I was drunk.

I rested for a while, or I should say "daydreamed", and then wrote the following poem. It's entitled "A Birthday Ode to Cindy" and I wrote it in preparation for her birthday that was only six weeks away. I knew in my heart that our reunion would take place on that day — her 23rd birthday. It did. I had the poem done in old english script on parchment paper and it became my first gift to my "found" daughter. It flowed from my heart as ink flows from a pen. It was there within me all the time waiting for the right moment to be expressed. That evening of May 28 was that moment. I now knew, not only her name, but had heard her voice as well. Soon I would see her face to face.

A Birthday Ode to Cindy

How do I begin to say
The things within my heart –
The many times I cried for you
Because we had to part.

How do I begin to tell
Of the longings down inside
To try to convey the love I feel
That goes so deep and wide.

The many nights I prayed to God
That someday we would meet –
And we'd talk about the missing years
While sharing a birthday treat.

To know your name and hear your voice
Has brought me joy untold –
And as we share and share and share
Our lives we will unfold.

My prayers have been answered,
Thank you, Lord!
You've been so good to me;
I've loved my daughter all along
And only You could see.

The years have come and the years have gone –
But Cindy you never knew –
The 22 birthdays I celebrated
And thought of only you.

But this birthday is different
Because we know it's true –
This is the first one I can say
CINDY, I LOVE YOU!

The days to follow were filled with an abundance of expectation and anticipation. Each day I waited for the mailman and expected that each phone call would be hers. Her letter arrived within the week with a color snapshot of herself. Immediately upon receiving it I took it to a local photo shop to have it enlarged. I asked them to please handle it with special care and explained why. I was so afraid of it getting lost and right then it was the only tangible thing I had. The enlargement was an 11 by 14 done on canvas which hangs proudly on my living room wall along with pictures of my other children.

In her letter she asked how tall I was as she is only five feet in height and was curious to know who she took after. I told her that I am five feet, four and one-half inches tall, but that her father's mother was rather short. In answer to my question about church, she informed that she had been raised in an Episcopalian Church. She shared a little bit about her two brothers and her relationship with her adoptive parents. She closed by saying, "Please tell all your kids that I said 'hi' and that we all will get together sometime". I cherish that letter because it was the first. Whatever we receive following a reunion for the first time is so meaningful. We seem to grasp onto these momentos out of fear that they, too, will somehow disappear and we'll again be left with nothing — except the memory.

I spoke to Cindy via telephone approximately four times between the time she first called me and my decision to visit her. It had been ten weeks since I first discovered her name and my desire to meet her was becoming stronger and stronger. I know now that I was not exhibiting the patience her mother had spoken of in her letter to me. During a phone conversation early in July, I joked with her about finding me on her doorstep. She remarked that her husband had suggested that possibility since he was sure she had inherited her persistence from me. The following day I wrote and told her to expect me on her "special day" — meaning, of course, her birthday — which at that time was only two weeks away.

In the coming days I went shopping for maternity clothes (she was five months pregnant with her first child), I had the poem framed, and then again, I waited for the big day. The labor pains of waiting to meet my daughter for the first time were certainly as real and severe as those of giving her birth!

At 5:30 p.m., July 18, 1977, Liz and I left New Jersey and headed for Maryland. We arrived in the area around 7:00. Liz was as nervous as I and between the two of us, we formed an uncomposed pair. As we pulled up to the house, my whole body began to shake. I silently began to pray that the Lord would give me composure, that He would calm my inner jitters, that He would give me the right words to say. I was totally beyond any power of my own. I knew if God could calm the raging sea, He could surely calm my raging nerves.

We nonchalantly (for all appearances) got out of the car. I went on ahead while Liz lagged behind. I knocked on the door — it opened — and there she was!! My beautiful, little, pregnant, darling daughter.

My first words were, "Do you know who I am?" (silly question!) "Yes, you're Sandy". I gave her a hug and what followed is blurred and fuzzy. I only know that we spent three pleasurable hours talking, laughing, and sharing. I felt as though I had known her all my life. We looked at pictures, talked about relatives, discussed our jobs, being pregnant, housecleaning; etc. laughed and joked about some physical traits. The evening was topped off by sharing the chocolate birthday cake I had baked and brought. She said it was her favorite kind, which pleased me since chocolate is also my family's favorite.

Here I was in my daughter's home with her husband and my adoptee friend, Liz, sharing her 23rd birthday! What words in the English language, or any other, could possibly describe the feeling of that evening. My spirit leapt within me as I gazed with wonderment on my full-grown child.

At approximately 11:00 p.m. we said our farewells and left Maryland with ecstatic feelings.

What Now, My Love?

The following afternoon I received a phone call from Cindy thanking me for the "beautiful" poem, complimenting me on my ability to write, and expressing more than once her gratitude for it. When we hung up I wrote her another long letter — thanking her for the warm visit and for the hospitality shown towards Liz and I. My heart was overflowing with love and in an attempt to restrain it, I mentioned that our relationship would be whatever she wanted it to be. Continuing contact was entirely up to her. She was going to be calling the shots! Little did I realize at that point that I was kidding myself.

During that week I called everyone I could think of who had known of my search and expounded upon my "fantastic" reunion with my long-lost daughter. In retrospect, I imagine I was reassuring myself that I had not been rejected and was anxious to prove that to everyone else.

A few days following the reunion, one of the girls I had gone to school with called me long distance from Illinois to tell me her mother had seen an article in the paper about me. Being one of the very few who stood by me in my time of need, she naturally was quite interested in what the intervening years had wrought. The sound of her voice took me back to early 1954 when thoughts of suicide were tiptoeing through my mind. "Sandy, the Lord will not give you any more than you are able to handle!" was the beautiful remark which came from this dear friend as I shared with her the weight of despair. It was good to hear from her again.

Throughout the week I felt as though I were floating through life on a big, white, fluffy marshmallow cloud. Everything was bright and beautiful.From the top of the mountain, the valley below was only a mirage. My impossible dream of 20 odd years had become a reality. Not only had I found her, but I had actually put my arms around her and kissed her!

Late in July, I called her at the office to see if she might want to meet me for lunch. She said, "Sure," and gave me directions. Since it was a 40-minute drive, I had little time to prepare and on the spur of the moment, I asked my two younger daughters if they would like to meet their sister. Sherri, 16, was excited at the idea and Linda, 17, was nonchalant, but both decided to go. When we arrived, she was ready and waiting for us. She introduced us to her boss and after the formalities, we were off to lunch.

I had hoped to go to a restaurant or diner, but was outnumbered by the younger generation and "fast food" it was! We chatted and laughed, especially when one of the girls said something about Cindy being so short and Dad being so tall — forgetting, of course, that they had different fathers.

When we got back to her office, we took a few snapshots which I cherish. I invited her and her husband, Ben to come to dinner some evening. She said she'd give me a call. Within a few weeks, we had set up a dinner date. I asked what her favorite dish was and set about getting the best recipe I could find. The day of the dinner, I spent nervously trying to make everything "just right". I cleaned as never before, brought out the best dishes, purchased a new lace tablecloth and awaited my royalty!

The waiting was unbearable. The minutes seemed to be hours. Finally they appeared. They had gotten lost (my terrible directions). Since everything was ready, we immediately sat down to eat. My youngest son, Steven discussed football with Cindy's husband while we girls talked about more important things.

Following the meal we retired to the living room. I couldn't wait to bring out the family album and I knew she couldn't wait to see all her blood relatives. Again, I was deceiving myself. It was at this point that I began to sense something was wrong. She had expressed no desire or interest and hardly paid any attention as I rattled off who was who. I then mentioned the fact that my younger sister was very eager to meet her since they were only a year apart in age. She startled me with the remark that, "I'd rather not meet anybody else. I want to cool the relationship." I can only recall being speechless and feeling uncomfortable. Speechless because I had not anticipated it and uncomfortable because now I was facing rejection and I wasn't sure how to handle it. I think I muttered something to the effect of, "Fine, you let me know when you're ready." The conversation that followed was shallow and brief. As they left, I could feel the mountaintop descending, merging into the valley, as the exhilaration drained from me.

A few days later I called just to "chat" and was told again that she wished to "cool" the relationship. When I asked if her parents were still upset, she said, "Yes", but also added, "with the baby coming, I think it would be too confusing for the child to have two maternal grandmothers".

I was finally beginning to see the handwriting on the wall. It was quite obvious that excuses were being given. It should have been obvious before, but I refused to face it. I asked if she minded me calling and she remarked that I could call occasionally. I then made one request of her – to please keep me informed about the baby. She promised that she would. This was the third week in August and she was due the middle of October. For the next two months, I steered clear of the phone or writing.

October came and went. No word. The beginning of November I took the plunge and called to see if she had had the baby. Ben answered and I expressed my concern. He said she still had not delivered and again promised to let me know. I remember wondering if I was being told the truth. Possibly they had no intentions of telling me anything about the baby. I realized that I was becoming paranoid. Rejection was looming heavy. The week of November 14, I began to call the hospital every day to see if she had been admitted. On the 17th, I was told that she had delivered the night before. Ironically, November 16, the date of my first grandchild's birth, was also my father's birthdate. That following Saturday I received a letter from her adoptive mother telling me about the baby and the difficulty Cindy had in delivering. She concluded her letter by saying, "I believe Cindy has made it clear that at this point and for the forseeable future, she does not wish to have a close or on-going tie with you and your family. I hope you will grant her that right."

My response follows verbatim:

Dear Mrs. Nanreit:

Thanks so much for your kind letter. It's such a relief to know that Cindy and baby are ok. I feel bad that she had a difficult time.

I intend to back out of Cindy's life as quietly and quickly as I entered. I hope that I have not caused any problems – my intention was only to express my love and concern. I am satisfied and happy to

57

know she has turned out so well — thanks to you.

As you stated so aptly, there is room in our lives for various relationships, but only if we choose to have them. I fully realize that we cannot force ourselves on others and I certainly do not wish to. You both know that I am here if and when either of you should want to call on me for whatever reasons. Thanking you again for keeping me informed.

Sandy

During the next several weeks I would question, reason, evaluate, rationalize and debate with myself the turn of events. How was it possible that the fantastic, beautiful, marvelous reunion had so suddenly disappeared into oblivion. Why God? Why did you open all those doors? Why did you allow me all that bliss, only to snatch it away? Why God? God did not respond — not immediately.

58

While my search was going on, I had begun meeting with other birthparents. We had formed a local branch called Concerned United Birthparents, Inc. This group had its beginnings in Massachusetts about a year before. It helped us to discuss our feelings, which certainly are unique to only those people who have surrendered a child for adoption. Our monthly meetings grew from only four at the first meeting to twenty-five in a three-month period.

Toward the end of November, a large local newspaper contacted me to see if they could do a story about C.U.B. Would I be willing? Yes, I would. I invited the journalist to attend the meeting which was to be held the following Sunday. When she arrived I announced to the group and anyone who wished to remain anonymous could. I requested that our C.U.B. address be given. Since I had made a decision to "go public", I wanted to know that others would have an avenue of making contact with us if they had the need to. As a result of that article, the letters began to pour in – heartbreaking, sad letters expressing pain, letters of appreciation for exposing the "other side" of the triangle.

Other newspapers began to call and wished to do similar articles I had refused to allow them to use a picture of Cindy, though they could photograph me or my children. The story was carried in several papers. Time passed. Late in January, a reporter from a large Philadelphia newspaper came to my home to interview me. My teenagers were all present hoping to get in on the action. However, the photographer thought a picture of me talking on the phone while looking at my daughter's picture would be quite appropriate for the story. I thought nothing much about it – until I saw it in print and again I questioned. "Why God? Why did you allow me to have that picture taken? Why, when I refused all the others?" The story even misquoted me in several instances. They stated that I was invited to my daughter's home when actually I had gone of my own volition. Why Lord?

Suddenly an answer came. It came through the scripture in Isaiah 55:8,9, which says, "This plan of mine is not what you would work out, neither are my thoughts the same as yours! For just as the heavens are higher than the earth, so are my ways higher than yours, and my thoughts than yours." This was the beginning of my acceptance of the "rejection" I was experiencing.

A few days after the newspaper hit the stands, Cindy called me. I had not had any conversation with her since late August. It was now late January – five months later. Anger was in her voice. She accused me of using her for my own gain. She said that while it was my story, it was not hers! I tried to explain that the picture was unintentional, but I inwardly knew the impossibility of convincing her of same. She made it quite clear that she was very unhappy with my decision to go public. I apologized for hurting her in any way and our discussion ended. The next day I was back to letter writing:

Dearest Cindy:

I am truly sorry for the distress I seem to have caused you. My main purpose of sharing my story was to help the whole cause of adoption.

Just recently I spoke at a hearing regarding the problem of children being placed and kept in foster care – and the total question as to why they have not been placed for adoption. My feeling concerning that issue is that most birthparents today do not want to completely break ties with their own flesh and blood children with the thought of never knowing anything about them or ever seeing them again; so they use the foster-care system to "hang on". It would seem to me that if the adoption system could be updated and that records could be opened to the adult adoptee, then possibly more parents would be willing to let go, knowing that it would not be "forever".

It's both interesting to me and ironic that there have been many reunions lately – all of which have been good. While I am naturally *hurt* over my own situation, I consider a much larger picture than just mine. I really have nothing to gain. I am not being paid for the number of hours I am spending for the "cause" – speaking, writing, coordinating this local chapter that is growing by leaps and bounds. However, I am *committed*. I believe in what I am doing.

While we are on the subject of feelings – I was extremely disappointed and upset that you were unable to convey to me the fact that you wanted no further contact. I would rather have heard it directly from you than from your mother. You are now an adult and I had hoped we could relate on that level. Obviously many of the signals that I either gave or received were misunderstood. I had a false impression following our first phone conversation and first meeting that you were as happy about our reunion as I. I now realize and have faced the fact that you were mainly interested in background information.

I don't know how to express my sorrow over your response. If there had been some communication between us, you would have realized how involved I was right from the start. Again, I am saddened that I have caused you any hurt. I can only ask for your forgiveness and let you know that it was not intentional.

Sandy

As I mourned my misfortune, the Lord kept speaking, "My thoughts are not your thoughts, nor are your ways, my ways". He kept reminding me that, as from the beginning, He was in complete control of the situation. While I did not understand it, I knew He was a God I could put my trust in and so I continued to "Cast my cares upon Him..." (I Peter 5:7.).

More and more letters were arriving. At first I started to answer each one personally until I found it necessary to send out a form letter about our group and attach a brief handwritten note to it. Later I sought the help of other girls in the group to respond personally to some of the heartrendering letters that continued to come.

At about this time, the Adoption Forum was planning their second annual conference. Being a board member and the representative birthparent, I was asked on several occasions to do some local T.V. talk shows in order to promote the conference. At this point I had nothing more to lose. I had "lost" my daughter for the second time and was now in the process of learning to deal with this new situation. The importance of keeping busy was paramount so as not to fall into the depths of depression where I would be no good to anyone. The T.V. publicity brought more letters and, of course, many more people into the organization. Many had stated that they never knew anyone else who had given up a child for adoption. It was refreshing for them to hear someone be so open, but how could they do it? They've never told another person about it! What would people say? How do they tell their children? We followed up on every phone call. No one was ever left without a listening, understanding and sympathetic ear.

Plans for the conference continued. I would be giving the workshop entitled "How To Deal With Giving Up A Child". Little did the participants know that there could have been a "twice" added to the end of that title.

Again God began to point out things to me. Things which we all innately know. It's easy to be in control, to be happy, to be together when things are going well, but how about when things aren't going so well. How about when events and circumstances are not to our liking? Can we still smile? Can we still look beyond and know that behind that cloud there *is* a silver lining — that the sun *still* shines, even though we can't see it? Again He gave me a scripture to back up my feelings. "When we run into problems and trials, we can rejoice for we know that they are good for us — they help us learn to be patient. And patience develops strength of character in us and helps us trust God more each time we use it until finally our hope and faith are strong and steady." (Romans 5:3,4.) I saw the evidence of this becoming a reality in my life. I knew that in order to be effective in the lives of others, I would need to "get it together". Only then could I lead, guide and direct those who had suffered the loss of a child through adoption.

Conference time arrived. The workshop room held 40 and it was full to capacity. Some people had to take another workshop because there just wasn't any more room. One couple came to me and asked if they could please attend because it was their whole purpose for being at the conference. I said, "Sure, but you'll have to stand." They agreed and also promised to register early next year.

A few days before the conference, I cut out a big red letter "A". I decided to use it as an attention-getter and also to make a point. I thought I'd practice on my kids, but when I held it up to my chest and asked them what they thought it stood for, I got all wrong answers. One thought it stood for "adoption", another thought I was an "A" student, and the other two said "anxious" and "ability". I began to wonder if it was going to serve the purpose for which I intended it.

As I attached the red letter to my black outfit, I asked if anyone in the room could relate to it. It was obvious, as they smiled and commented to one another, that they did. Many of us who have had a child outside the "proper" bounds have been able to put ourselves in the classic novel "The Scarlet Letter". We've all been there. We know the feeling of glaring eyes, soft whispers, pointed fingers. No, we didn't have to stand on a platform in the middle of town. It was much more subtle than that! I expressed to the group my own feeling that if I had robbed a bank or even killed in passion, I would not have been as condemned as that of a "fallen" woman. The imprint of the scarlet letter had been burned into my soul.

We shared our various experiences before turning our attention to the purpose of the workshop: How To Deal With Giving Up A Child. I prepared and gave the following outline which I learned in the School of Life — Bachelor's Degree earned — still working on Master's.

How To Deal With Giving Up A Child

Giving up a child and then learning to live with that decision is not easy — in fact, it's extremely difficult. It's a day-by-day ongoing experience which never stops, not even after a reunion. At the same time, however, growth can be acquired — if that's what we really want. I have personally applied the following principles to every area of my life and found them to be workable. It is my sincere desire and prayer that anyone who is suffering the misery of hopelessness and despair will consider these principles as suggested cures and follow the remedies to a new way of life.

Love that Heals (agape)

Our first and foremost responsibility is to *will* not to blame others. As birthparents it's so easy for us to lay the blame elsewhere. Our parents, the social workers, the doctors, the lawyers, the judges, all could be directly responsible for our pain. While that may be true, the above says that we are going to *will* not to blame others. We are going to (maybe for the first time ever) say to ourselves, "I did what I had to do at that point in time with the circumstances which were surrounding me". It's o.k. to say, "I would do it differently today knowing what I know now". The point of the matter is, we must be able to admit that we did what we had to do at the time, since, in most instances, we had no other options. Then we can begin a healing process. While we cannot control the actions or conduct of other people, we can control our reaction and our response to their conduct. We need to replace anger, bitterness and hate with compassion, understanding and love. As we gave so much of ourselves in the giving of our children, we need to continue with that love in order to

63

come through our experience as healthy individuals. That does not mean that righteous anger does not have its place. It does. That is the purpose of getting involved in an organization like C.U.B., or any of the other adoption groups that are constructuvely working to exert change. Channel your anger to a worthwhile cause — humanizing adoption.

Most of us surrendered our children because we were convinced at the time that they would have a better chance at life. Let us continue to make love our aim so that when reunion time rolls around, they will not find us unhappy, hostile, bitter people who they would not want to align themselves with. Let's continue to believe that love will find a way.

Faith that Heals (complete trust and confidence)

What is it that we fear? Often we cannot answer that question because we are not in touch with our feelings. Childhood is laden with controls built on instilling fear. Sometimes the process is so subtle that when we reach adulthood we don't know why we fear what we do. One thing is certain: fear is a formidable giant. It can control and dominate our every thought and action. More often than not, it is irrational and destructive and is laid upon us under the label of control, wisdom and safety. We need to ask if this is really the case. Then we need to expose these repressed hurts of the past. As we do, we can expect intense inner pain, but these hurts need to be brought to the surface before we can deal with them. Just as an open wound heals more quickly when exposed to the air, so will our fears and hurts of the past.

Oftentimes we develop a defense mechanism that keeps us from facing up to our problems. When our insecurity compels us to put up a wall, it not only keeps out our enemies, but it also denies entrance to our friends.

Inner healing needs to be done in a context of loving people who care and understand. That is the reason for the success of self-help groups that are sweeping our country. People who have had similar experiences can relate to us much more quickly than someone who has not walked the same path.

One of the common fears that most of us have is that if anyone should find out about us, they would reject us. This is especially true of birthparents because of society's condemnation of the past. This type of fear causes us to live in a constant state of tension.

A positive attitude will bring a positive result. Ongoing trust and confidence is the highway to wholeness. No matter what old negative ghosts return to haunt us, we are assured by faith that they will pass.

Surrender that Heals (to give over or yield)

Birthparents are very familiar with this word. In this context we are going to use it to mean the surrender of self-destructive patterns, such as hate, fear, resentment and jealousy. These attitudes are enslaving. It is only when we can admit to ourselves, "I need and want help," that inner healing can begin. Surrender is an ongoing and progressive act — it demands that we look at our destructive patterns and see their deadly potential.

Forgiveness that Heals

Forgiveness is at the very heart of inner healing. It is so necessary to deal with unforgiveness before hidden bitterness can be exposed and transformed. Again, if our emotions cannot respond with forgiveness, *our will can*. We need to forgive the hardest of all persons to forgive — ourselves. When we forgive ourselves, we will then begin to like ourselves — only then can be begin to love everyone else. When we finally accept imperfections in ourselves, we react less severely to the faults of others.

Confession that Heals (acknowledgement)

Confession is simply an act of honest exposure. It is always therapeutic. There is something refreshing and disarming about one who has nothing to hide. One of the rules of conduct in A.A. is absolute honesty. There is no hope of inner healing if we insist on living a lie. Human dignity cannot exist without honesty. We bury our guilt and the cost of it can be unbearably high. It takes its toll on body and mind. I personally know of many birthparents who are suffering physical pain which I believe to be a direct result and cause of buried guilt and their inability to deal with it. The synonym for sickness is dis-ease (a lack of inner peace). The destruction of emotional ease because of hidden guilt is probably the number one destroyer of health — both body and mind.

As we expose our hearts to one another and gain acceptance, there is no need for us to return to the chains that once held us in bondage. It is truth that will make us free! What we affirm today, we will become tomorrow.

Another thing that confession does is to clear the mind. When we have nothing in our mind which seems to deserve punishment, there is no fear. We can then given unconditional love because that is what we want for ourselves.

Self-Acceptance that Heals (to believe in self)

The home, the school, our peer group, the church, etc. all demand conformity to one set of values. Because of this we become like a collàge composed of the demands from all these varied emotional pressure groups.

It is our self-image — *not* our circumstances, which is the primary source of our anxiety — the cancer of self-condemnation. When we as birthparents stop condemning ourselves, come forth in confidence with constructive ideas toward change, then I believe that is what we will see — change. First we've got to improve our self-acceptance and our internal attitudes. The external circumstances will begin to change as a result.

The need of unconditional love can emanate only from a person who has been broken and reconstructed. It's that person who has compassion for other broken people and can accept you no matter what you have done. If you are still struggling with your self-image, you need to take some affirmative action toward wholeness. A good place to start is by learning, repeating, and living The Serenity Prayer. It's simple, brief, and powerful. It goes like this:

> God, grant me the serenity (inner peace)
>   to accept the things I cannot change,
> The courage to change the things I can,
> And the wisdom to know the difference.

There are some things that just cannot be changed. Those things we need to learn to accept. There are many things that can be changed and we need the courage and fortitude to change them. Lastly, we need the wisdom to recognize the difference between those things that we can't change and those things that we can. Self is the best place to start.

Section II — Personal Case Histories

"... what it really means is that the parent cares for her child so much she will give up her own wish and desire to have her own offspring with her in order to benefit the child. These are the real moralists of our day. Very few people in any strata of life have the morality of parents who were forced to give up the child under duress and since then have voluntarily restrained themselves from fighting and saying, 'I want to have that kid'. They are people who sacrifice in a way that most of us don't know how to sacrifice. There is a tremendous humanity there which can be used to serve the child and to serve us, too."

— John L. Brown, "Rootedness",
FAMILY INVOLVEMENT, May/June 1974.

Others Who "Surrendered"

It's interesting to note as I begin this section that social workers, psychiatrists, psychologists, judges, lawyers, etc., have all seen fit to speak for the birthparent. Until recently, few have ever asked us to speak for ourselves. At the time of relinquishment, we were told that we would have other children. We could start a new life, and no one need ever know about our past. They never bothered to check back and see how we had fared over the years. If they had, they would have then realized that signing one's name to a piece of paper does not begin to erase all the emotional and deep feelings involved with giving birth.

The following stories have been included in order to convey to you, the reader, the fact that my story is not unique. While each story is different because of the circumstances surrounding it, all are basically the same. The same thread of hurt, pain, confusion, sadness, wondering, permeate the life of each birthparent.

While these birthparents now have good family relationships and other children, they still harbor many unresolved feelings about the child they surrendered. We use the word "surrender" because that's what we had to do. We found ourselves in a position where the only thing we could do was to "give up" or "yield". To surrender means that you've got no other way out. Things are closing in and about you and your only survival seems to be to surrender. It's seldom, if ever, done willingly.

It gives us a sense of freedom to be able to discuss our deep-felt emotions. Under the guise of our protection, the courts have used us as an excuse to keep our children and their roots locked up forever. Though many of us are now speaking out, we're still being called the minority.

Why is is that more and more young girls are keeping their babies than ever before? Could it be that they do not wish to bear the pain of having to give up their own flesh and blood, never to see that child again? Increasing numbers of birthparents are returning to their social agencies seeking information about the children they relinquished. It is their desire to update the facts about themselves and to have the information placed in the record. They want to be available to their birthchild if they should ever want to find them. These parents have *never* forgotten the child they gave up.

The people who have shared the following stories with me are caring people. They are concerned about their child's welfare, their child's well-being and their child's concerns. As you read these stories, be mindful of the pressures that were involved and the time period that each took place. Try to put yourself into the story and maybe then you will be that much closer to understanding what it means to part with a child — to part with one's own flesh and blood. Those who have experienced the death of a loved one have some small inkling of the birthparents' plight. There are times when even death would have been easier to accept. The illustration of the M.I.A.s is probably a better parallel. Their families never know if their soldier kin are alive somewhere or dead. They live on with the hope of someday finding out. As birthparents, we can relate to that feeling so well. We never know what happened to the children we gave birth to. But today as never before, we have hope. We are beginning to see a faint light at the end of the tunnel and with each passing day it becomes brighter, pulling us toward our reunion day.

Chris — Age 42

As a young girl of 20 and desperately in love, I would have followed this man to the ends of the earth, but when I found out I was pregnant, that is where the earth ended. Even before I knew about it, my baby's father had already become engaged to someone else. He, of course, was not too happy to hear of my pregnancy, and first he suggested abortion, which I would not have agreed to, and I never mentioned marriage because I knew better.

I found a maternity home about 100 miles from my home where I went to stay for five months to await the birth of my baby. When he was born, he was beautiful and I couldn't keep away from the nursery window, just watching him sleep.

We returned to the "Home" together where I fed, dressed, loved and rocked him for three short weeks. The morning he was to leave to go to his new home, I ached inside knowing each time I touched his hair and kissed his face it was probably for the last time. When the final moment arrived I dressed him in his new clothes sent by his new mother, and carried him to the door where, the nurse took him from me and with a nod of her head saying "nevermore", he disappeared.

That afternoon I was on the train home. I cried, hated and loved. I cried for myself, loved my son and hated all the stupid reasons I had to give him to someone else. There never was any counseling given to me other than, "This is the right thing for his sake. He will have everything. You don't want others calling him 'Bastard'."

I went on with my life, marrying, having three other children, but never being able to forget my first child. Each birthday, I baked a cake and cried and celebrated within myself, wondering where

71

could he be, is he dead, is he happy? Who does he look like? Does he know he is adopted, does he hate me?

As the years went by, articles started appearing in papers and magazines. With each one I read, I hoped someday I would see my son again. In January 1978, I wrote to ALMA (Adoptees Liberty Movement Association) hoping, since my son was now 21 years old, he had registered there. But he hadn't. Then I read about CUB and how wonderful it was to know that all the feeling and hurt and wondering was normal and I felt an inward release of guilt. In March I found an Adoptee Search Group in the city where I live and I finally found someone I could talk to that understood how I felt.

With the help of these wonderful friends, I found my son, who I contacted after much mind searching, because I didn't want to hurt him and I didn't know how he would feel. The day after he received my letter, he phoned me and we talked for a long time and before he hung up he said he wanted to thank me for giving him life and for having the courage to search for him. Now we have exchanged pictures and tapes and letters and love.

We are making arrangements for a reunion because there is quite a distance between where we live. But now I feel whole and complete again and very soon I will once again touch his hair, hold his face in my hands, kiss him and tell him "I love you".

Rosemarie — Age 23 (the youngest to tell her story)

The furthest thing from my mind in 1972 was falling in love — especially with a high school sweetheart. I usually kept to myself since I always felt like a misfit and I associated mostly with older people. We were just good friends at first, but over a period of time we became very close.

He proposed to me on March 6, 1972, and I believe that's when I conceived our child — he was only 16½ and I was 17½. I tried to squelch the suspicions that cropped up within me, but finally I went for a pregnancy test. Suspicions became reality and when finally going to our parents, with fear racing through us, they tried to talk us into abortion. We could not bring ourselves to do it because we loved the "little babe" within me.

We started job hunting so we could save up enough money for an apartment because I had every intention of keeping my child. I got a job in a factory doing tedious work under bad lighting and surrounded by loud motors and compressors. It wasn't the best job, but I was desperate. We found an apartment in Philadelphia, an efficiency, which was badly in need of paint. A few friends helped and were very sympathetic towards us — even to the point of offering to lend us money — so for a while we seemed to be "on top of things". Everything seemed to be working out until it was time for me to take maternity leave.

I started making the rounds in an effort to get some financial aide. Welfare told me that I needed parental consent and would not help me. I was then humbled to the point of begging in three of Philadelphia's largest hospitals for some sort of prenatal counseling and some place to deliver my baby. It seemed as though the whole world was heartless. All they wanted me to do was to have an abortion!

I thought I better try to find SOMEONE who could refer me to an agency. Not for the purpose of adoption, but just for some prenatal care and a roof over my head as my apartment was becoming a financial burden. I talked to my old high school counselor. He put me in touch with Child Care Services. One of the caseworkers made the rounds of clinics with me for more tests — more expenses — more wear and tear on our hearts — but no answers!

One of the maternity homes refused to help me unless I had parental consent. I tried to explain my fears of telling my parents, but they would not listen. I tried to be strong, but ended up in tears begging for help. Ed and I were beginning to realize our impending defeat. We decided we had no option other than to tell my parents and see what would happen. What we suspected would happen, happened. They were dead set against us getting married. All they were concerned about was what the neighbors would say, etc. From that day until the day I went to a home for unwed mothers, I was kept inside so no one would see me. My parents tried to convince me that it was best for me to go into the home and started to talk about adoption. I had no intentions of giving up my child, but rather than argue with them, I planned to fight it from within the Home through the caseworkers.

They treated me fairly well. I had prenatal care and labor/delivery classes. I took some courses to keep me busy and even contributed to the Home's newsletter.

I tried to confront my mother with the why's and wherefore's of adoption when she visited, but she just kept on saying, "You have to — you just have to!" She seemed to age 15 years right before my eyes — which only fed my guilt.

On December 10, 1973, at 4:30 a.m., I delivered a beautiful six pound, three ounce baby boy. Ed and I named him David Christopher. I insisted on feeding and holding him and was permitted to do so. I kissed him, played with him, and prayed for him. Whenever the nurse would bring him to me, he'd stretch out his arms to me and whenever they'd come to take him back, he'd grab hold of my nightgown and start to cry. I wonder if he somehow knew our separate fates.

Ed went to a Christian bookstore and bought a gold cross on a chain for David which had a message of our love for him on it. I pleaded with God for a way to keep my beloved child — either that or death. God chose not to answer that prayer.

The day before I was to leave the hospital, I stayed up most of the night crying. I finally went to sleep around 4:00 and woke up about 6:00. I got dressed and went down to the nursery to say my last good-bye. At first they weren't going to let me hold him, but I insisted, and was permitted to do so. Ed came in while I was holding him and we both started crying. The nurse came and took him away – it was though she had taken part of me with her.

We had to go to a relinquishment hearing which was and is a farce of our judicial system. We were not in full agreement with the proceedings. Laws are slowly being changed. I would personally like to see some laws passed protecting the rights of young mothers who really want to keep their babies.

I feel that this trauma has left permanent wounds and change in us. We married a year and a half later in 1975. The loss of our first-born son stays with us and we live in the hope of being reunited with him when he reaches majority age. In the meantime, we hope and pray for strength, and for the present adoption system to be changed.

The following poem, along with the gold cross went with David to his adoptive home (at least we were told that it would).

I'll take you home with me, my love,
if only in my heart.
I'll watch you grow, and love, and learn,
even though we are apart.

My babe, my precious jewel, my own,
please try to understand
I wanted to keep you to myself,
but God had another plan.

He meant for you and I to part –
to bring two people joy –
And he picked you above all the rest,
my darling little boy.

David, dear, I love you so
and it causes me much pain
To say goodbye, but I know my loss
will be another's gain

I'll never forget the times we had
when I held you as you slept
And I'll still feel sad and lonely
though many tears I've wept.

75

I Would Have Searched Forever

I love you, David, with all my heart
I guess I always will
And when we part, there'll be a place
  that only you can fill.

But darling, as I hold you
I'm trying not to cry
But it's just so hard to hold back tears
  when I'm saying my last goodbye.

(Written December 14, 1973)

Jackie — Age 28 (married the birthfather)

My son, Mark, born on September 5, 1968, is the fruit of a very young and beautiful love affair. A love that still grows after eight years of marriage. Yet, the fruit of this love ripens elsewhere. Mark was relinquished for adoption at the age of one month.

Bill and I started dating when I was fourteen and he was just shy of seventeen. Love came very easily to us, and as our love deepened, we found the intimate expressions of love very natural and beautiful. We were naive, yet realized the possibility of a pregnancy. A child conceived through our love was not upsetting to us. And Mark was conceived in December of my senior year in high school when I was seventeen.

The world fell apart when our families were told about my pregnancy. Tragically, we could not put the pieces back once they fell. It seemed, then, everyone knew what we should do with our lives, and they made sure we were informed of their "wise" opinions. The pressure was tremendous and my mind was a maze of questions and doubts. These doubts led me to cancelling my wedding date and to doubting my love for Bill. The only constant in my life was my baby. I loved my child and no one could alter that love in any way. Billy, (my son's birthname), became the focal point of my life. His needs and his wellbeing came first. I guess maternal instinct came easily to me also. The sad fact is that I was made to believe that this was not enough — that I was not enough for my own son. I loved him with every ounce of my being, yet, no one knew the depths of that love.

It was a combination of this factor and people who influenced me, or more accurately stated, gently coerced me into placing my child for adoption. To this day I feel these people do not realize what they had asked of me.

The love and pain remain; something that was not mentioned when the adoption was being considered. I was told, "You're young — you'll have other children," as if one child could replace another. I have four beautiful little girls. Mark has four sisters, but there is a very special part of my heart that belongs to my firstborn. I have learned painfully that time does not heal all! Much of the time I am anguished. My grief is undescribable.

Last winter I came to the point in my life where depression controlled my life. I was in the depths of depression — a prisoner of my own emotions. I could not find the key to unlock the door. For so long I had tried to suppress my grief. I tried to continue with my quiet life when my whole being was screaming inside. I didn't even realize the source of my depression. I sought professional counsel, and this helped me to function again. Still, I was very unhappy and unsettled. I don't know how or when, but I became acutely aware of the basis of my emotional state. I finally realized the adoption had taken place for no good reason. And now I grieve! I allowed myself to grieve!

Somewhere in this grief the Lord touched me. He touched me through "Concerned United Birthparents". I am no longer alone in my grief. There are others who truly understand and share my grief. Through this sharing came knowledge and courage.

After attending my first CUB meeting I called the agency and arranged an appointment with the social worker who had handled my case. I knew what I wanted. I was absolutely sure what was right this time. I wanted Mark to know the circumstances of his birth and adoption. I wanted him to know of my love. I was welcomed warmly and assured that Mark's file would be opened to him upon request when he reaches majority age. I was given some peace that day. Tears of joy flowed upon learning my son's first name. How beautiful! I was given some precious information about his babyhood. I know he has wide feet. He has feet like mine! I am thrilled; he is a little like me. Now I know he is happy, healthy and loved. I thank God for this knowledge.

Now I am working towards establishing contact with Mark's family through the agency. I do not want to intrude in their lives, but Mark and I still have needs. He needs to have answers to his questions. I believe his emotional well-being demands that they be answered when they are asked. As for me, I need to know of Mark. I need to know how he is growing, and I need a picture. I can't go on searching strange faces and hoping to find one I'll recognize. I need a face for this child I love.

There is no happily ever after for this story. But there is hope. A hope that some day Mark will understand and accept my love. Perhaps he will even love in return.

I love you Mark!

Irene — Age 48

It was on my 26th birthday in 1957, that my son, John, was conceived. Although I was a late bloomer, circumstances saw to it that I was still unmarried when actually at the age of 25 something deep inside me stirred with the desire to be a mother.

So it was that after an unhappy love affair with someone else, I found myself being pursued by my boss, who was in the throes of a marital breakup (nothing to do with me). If I hadn't been so lonely, with no date on my birthday, I might not have accepted his invitation to dinner, etc. Being flattered by his attention, and being somewhere between caring for him a great deal and compassion, the inevitable happened. So it was that on our first union, I conceived.

I left my job as executive secretary to go into seclusion. I stayed at the home of a schoolteacher girlfriend and cared for her daughter while waiting for my baby to be born. Realizing I could not keep my son, I made plans for his adoption through another friend who worked for a lawyer.

I lacked the courage to tell my parents in those "unenlightened" years, feeling it would break their hearts to know the truth. In the meantime, my sister found out just before I gave birth and tried to persuade me to keep the baby. By then the adoption plans had been laid and I didn't feel I had the right to go back on my word to the lawyer who had arranged everything. My hospital expenses and doctor fees were being paid by the adopting parents as I hadn't enough money to pay for them myself. Accordingly, I felt I had to go ahead with the adoption.

My son was born on August 10, 1958. While in the hospital, I was informed by a kind social worker that I could see my baby —

much to my surprise. I did feed my son, held him, and talked to him for nearly a week. It was with mixed feeling and much regret that I gave him up. However, I felt at the time that he would have a better life with a complete family, which included a father.

The following year I was married, and am still married to the same man. I have a son and daughter. My children have kept me quite busy and my mind occupied most of the time. However, I have never forgotten the child I gave up for adoption. He is now of legal age. I have wondered if he'd like to find me. I am willing to be found, but do not want to pursue the search for fear of upsetting him or the adoptive parents. I know that they have undoubtedly made all the sacrifices one makes as a parent and he belongs to them, but as he becomes his own caretaker, I would like so much to know how he is and whether he has a good and happy life. I would also like to be able to explain why I felt the necessity to give him up for adoption.

The lawyer who handled my case is now deceased. I have been in touch with another lawyer who has taken over the affairs of the first. He informed me that my son was adopted in Maryland, but could not or would not give me any further information.

I am presently living in southern New Jersey and it is my sincere hope, desire, and prayer that someday I may extend the hand of friendship to my son.

Linda – Age 32

"What's a nice girl like you doing in a place like this?" asked the voice on the TV commercial as a woman was trying to clean out her dirty oven. I was sitting in a home for unwed mothers watching this and wondering what I was doing there. The following is my account of bearing a child out of wedlock.

My life had become stagnant. My boyfriend said our relationship was over. In turn I renewed a relationship with a man I had known for several years. This was to have a profound affect on my life.

In June I left for Hawaii disappointed in love and in search of excitement. At the end of July I suspected I was pregnant. The doctor confirmed it. I told him that marriage was not an option. One of his first questions was to ask what race my child would be. I didn't realize it but I was carrying a very desirable baby – a Caucasian. He said abortion would be psychologically damaging, but he knew a couple who would want my baby. I left his office numb and never returned.

After a while I contacted the birthfather by letter, but he was not interested in marriage. I had to go it alone. I was even afraid to tell my parents who never were very approachable. However, may I add that I should have humbled myself and asked my family for help. I believe that they would have had more sincere and genuine interest in my wellbeing than those from whom I sought help.

Hesitantly, I confided about my pregnancy to a fellow I had known from Pennsylvania who was stationed at Hickam Air Force Base. He felt life and birth were very sacred and told me I should be the mother of my own child.

I went to California where I rented a cottage near the Pacific

83

Ocean. I lied and pretended my husband was away on military duty. I even went so far as to go to a 5-and-10-cent store and bought a wedding ring for about $1.99.

I found work in a cafeteria, but after a month, the owner, who was Chinese, asked if I were pregnant. He said, "You take good care — maybe your child be President of the U.S." A flattering firing!

When I lost my job, I had an abundance of time to fill. I read everything in the library about birth and child rearing. I wanted to prepare myself for birth and motherhood. My feeling for this child growing inside me was intense. She was not planned, but she was wanted by me. I know in retrospect that she was not a mistake because God does not make mistakes.

I returned to Hawaii at the advice of a friend. She had contacted a maternity home. By this time I was five months pregnant. The social worker asked me what I wanted to do about the baby and if I had considered adoption. I didn't know what to do, but that was the first, but not the last time, I would hear the word "adoption". She too was very interested that I was going to have a Caucasian baby. She sent my name to a private adoption agency. This started my journey down the "Road to Adoption".

I stayed with a family in what was called a wage home. I was given room and board in turn for babysitting and household chores. I went back to the maternity home for pre-natal care by doctors from the hospital. I was required to stay at the maternity home before delivery.

One day I received a call from a man who announced that he was my social worker. He said he was to help me decide what was best for me and the baby. He delved deeply into my less than desirable home life as a child and adolescent. I was in a very emotional state. Much of the interview I was sobbing and hysterical. He said that because I had had a very sterile childhood, I deserved happiness now. The baby would encumber me. I pleaded that I would be a good mother. I never had any other options except adoption presented to me. That was his answer to my problem. Get rid of the baby and all would be fine. I could get married and have other children. He said I would be selfish to keep the baby. I had no fight — I was child and he was parent.

On February 29, I gave birth to a nine pound baby girl. The physical pain was shortly forgotten, but the emotional pain did linger. In the labor room a sign was posted on my bed which said "For Adoption." The type of delivery was never discussed with me by the doctors. I went through natural childbirth unprepared until moments before the baby was born. Then an injection was put into my spine. The baby was born, cried, and taken away. I did not see her then. I had to ask the nurse if my baby was whole and normal and what sex. They left me alone, unattended and unstrapped before I was taken to my room. I attempted to get up and almost fell except I caught myself on the pole of the I.V.

The next day I walked nervously down the corridor alone to see my daughter for the first time. I named her Devon. I looked and cried...

I even received flowers from the social worker at the adoption agency congratulating me. After three days I left the hospital. When I was to leave, I started to sob and cry. A nurse put her arm around me to comfort me. Unfortunately there was always someone to hold your hand or put their arm around you so you would be strong. I wish I would have been just able to cry and cry and get it over. My daughter went to a foster home. I did not know where; I didn't know I had the right to know.

I saw my daughter for the last time two weeks later at the agency. I bought two outfits for her. I remember when the salesgirl asked if she could help me I said, "I want to buy something for my daughter." I picked out a blue gingham slack set with mushrooms appliqued and a green sunsuit with ruffles. I held Devon in my arms. The first time I had ever held a brand new baby. She was all wrapped up in a blanket. I undid the blanket and saw her scaly feet and expressed concern. I was simply told not to worry.

I was told many details about the adoptive family. They sounded super and rich. However, now I think that they glorified the family to enhance their reasons why my daughter should be adopted. I was told that I loved her so much which is why I allowed her to be adopted.

I do love her very much – then and now – but that is not why she was adopted. The social worker gave me the words to put in my mouth which was rationalization. Society branded me bad and shameful. The social worker pressed for adoption. On March 19, papers were signed. She was theirs.

The agency dropped me. I did not hear from them unless I initiated a phone call. I asked for a picture of Devon. "NO!" I should have thought of that before. I was hysterical. The social worker snapped, "Go get yourself a lawyer!"

Now, it was time to start my new life – but was I prepared?

Barbara — Age 34

I am writing as an orphaned parent to express my loss and concern for my child, Kimberly Ann, as her original birth certificate read. She was born to me after a pregnancy filled with turmoil, uncertainty and wandering on my part.

Before her conception I had been living with her father. At that time I was a social worker for a large city agency in probation and parole. During our year together I was very much in love with her father although our backgrounds, values, and interests were very different. My family was unhappy and I was encountering much social conflict and personal despair (he was a lower-class black militant and petty hoodlum and I was a religious upper-middle-class white).

At this time in my life a man who I had known for years contacted me and began encouraging me to come to another state where he was sure I would enjoy life in a community of young people there and where I could find another interesting job. He had always expressed a serious interest in me and I was convinced he sincerely cared for me.

By the time I left in May of 1969, I suspected that I might be pregnant and I informed the natural father. He was distressed and tried to persuade me to remain with him. Since I had already made my plans (resigned my job, etc.), I followed through with them though I did not want to.

When arriving in the new city, I found a different situation than I had envisioned. My friend did everything possible to make me dependent upon him. There were no jobs available and I was feeling very pregnant. He was aware of my condition and assumed it was his

87

child as he had visited with me the last week in March and we had been intimate at that time. He had no knowledge of how I had been living and I did not know if my expected baby would be black or white. My parents had no idea I was pregnant and I could not bring myself to tell them without knowing which of the two men was the father.

In early October 1969, my "friend" with whom I was then living as common-law wife, decided to move. He had no knowledge of the area except that a former Marine buddy lived there. I had been getting the best of physical care while with him and we were becoming emotionally dependent upon each other so I went along.

The obstetrician I began seeing there set the due date for January 1, 1970. On the morning of November 28, 1969, my "husband" took me to the hospital where the baby was born five hours later. As she was being delivered, I could see her black hair and dark coloring. She was healthy and I was thrilled beyond words as I suppressed my fear of the agony I knew was ahead. No one mentioned anything about her being darker than the other babies in the nursery until two days later when the pediatrician came to talk with me. I told him the whole story and he was incredulous and concerned. By the time it was time to bring the baby home, my husband knew the truth. I felt horrible as he had looked forward to the baby being "his" and, of course, I had been deceiving him.

The pediatrician had been doing everything to think of a way for me to hold my family together. When the baby had been home about a week, we made an appointment to see a psychiatrist for counseling. By that time my husband told me that there was no way the situation could be worked out and I would not be able to keep "the little nigger".

Kimberly had cried all night every night since we had brought her home. She was eating poorly and continuing to lose weight so I was a nervous wreck. I must have known what was coming that evening when we went to see the psychiatrist, but I had not allowed myself to recognize it. After talking for a while with the doctor and my husband, I handed my bundle to a nurse in that ground-floor room of the hospital. That was December 10, 1969. I signed some temporary papers and later learned that she was kept at the hospital for several days before being placed in a black foster home. I believe I was later told this was a black attorney's home.

One day early in January I received a telephone call from an attorney asking that my husband and I come to his office that evening to sign the final papers for her adoption. We did so. No social worker or other person had contacted us during the interim to discuss what was happening. On the afternoon of the day the attorney called, I went to see Sister Diane, the administrator of the catholic hospital. This was at the attorney's suggestion when I told him I didn't know what was happening and how upset I was. Sister Diane was most understanding and, as she had personal knowledge of my child, told me that the welfare department was offering to accept relinquishment of my child. She warmly told of the foster care situation and seemed to believe that there would be little difficulty in finding a Christian adoptive home for her.

As I now look back, I cannot believe that I ever thought or felt as if I could not take care of my child. I know that much of my motivation was to protect my mother and father and others close to me from the disgrace, etc. My father is and was emotionally ill. This manifested itself in blaming my mother for everything imaginable and extreme racism, anti-semitism and ridiculously high and conforming expectations of me and my younger brother. I knew that his learning of my black child would result in his complete rejection of her and escalation of the blame upon my mother. I loved my mother so much – I didn't want to see this happen.

Why I felt I had to accept my "husband's" decision that I must be separated from Kim, I do not know. I just felt totally helpless and there was nowhere I could turn for help. I was extremely guilt-ridden and dependent upon him that I was simply out of my mind. It is strange that none of the "professionals" involved in the relinquishment ever mentioned to me that there might be an alternative to consider. It is strange that none of them had any doubt that I owed my first loyalty to a husband who had no sympathy for me.

The reason I finally signed the relinquishment was mainly that I had become convinced that a great many people could provide Kim with more than I could.

Throughout this period I spent my days and nights praying and crying. Everyone involved knew how devastated I was to be losing my baby. Some weeks after I signed the papers a social worker from the welfare department asked to talk to me to obtain a social history. At last someone recognized that Kim has a natural father too! I went to the office and told her about myself and Kim's father. She called late in March, 1970 and told me that Kim had been placed in a permanent adoptive home. The total information that I was given was that the adoptive parents were white and had other natural children. The one thing I had stressed to Sister Diane was that I wanted her in a strong Christian home. No one ever felt that they

89

could tell me the religious affiliation of the family, however.

In December 1969, I contacted the natural father to tell him he had a healthy baby daughter. He was helpless as I would not tell him where we were. When he finally found out what had happened to her, years later, he was heartbroken.

Within a week of the time I left Kim at the hospital my life began a fantastic downhill spiral — from being abused personally in every manner by my husband to having my family lend him thousands of dollars he would never repay and permitting him to cut me off from all outside contacts. He destroyed all my possessions and my few treasured momentos of Kim. I was undeniably a very sick woman. My husband's inability to support us or live within our means led him to move in August of 1970 (closer to my parents' money). Before long, however, this proved to be an error on his part. My parents could see that something was wrong and within weeks my mother had guessed quite accurately what had happened. Her sympathy for her "son-in-law" fast faded as she observed his treatment of me. Her feelings about the baby quickly resolved themselves and we comforted each other with the thought that even if we could not personally assure Kim would have all we wanted for her, at least she had an existence.

Late in 1970 as my husband came to realize that I no longer needed his abuse to punish myself and would be leaving him, he dramatically informed my father how I had ruined his life with the little nigger and what a whore I was. The expected results were obtained. My father has since lived in our family home in retirement completely withdrawn from my mother, brother and myself.

About this same time I was hired as a social worker. When I arrived for work the first day, I learned that my position would be in adoptions. I was a little bit stunned by the idea, but soon very enthusiastic as I wanted to learn as much as I could. There was no orientation or in-service training and as I had no formal education in social work, I was worried about the quality of service I was providing. Over the years I learned a great deal about adoption — how drastically different childrens' environments and destinies could be. This added knowledge and day-to-day reminders of my own experience. I never told my fellow social workers about my child. Many of the young women I worked with concerning the relinquishment of their babies touched me deeply. My agony had been anything but unique. This was something that only the minority of adoptive parents seemed to comprehend the extent of.

Over the past years I have kept in constant contact with the agency that handled Kim's adoption in attempts to learn how my child is doing. I especially inquired about the religious background of the adoptive family. I received a reply from the director of the agency telling me that Kim had been adopted by a "carefully selected" family and was receiving the necessary love and care. The letter went on to say I should know better than inquire further.

I've also kept in contact with Sister Diane on a yearly basis. She informs me that Kim is happy and well cared for. This is enough for my mother to know about her only grandchild, but I'm afraid my love is not so selfless and confident. But then I've seen a four year old beaten into a coma by his adoptive mother of eight months (placement into this loving home by the county welfare department). However, I do believe I can take Sister Diane's statements as her honest perception of the situation. However, I also have no reason to believe she has necessarily considered all aspects. I have never had reason to believe that Kim's family has any knowledge of her natural families. Surely a half-black child who may be growing up in a white world is going to need some information. Surely it will be easier for her or her adoptive parents to obtain than it is proving for me. But if just one link in her chain of information is unwilling – ?

One other incident comes to mind regarding a contact I've had with an agency about my child. Five months after her birth I received a routine inquiry in the mail from the Department of Health who had registered her birth. It gave the information as listed in their records and asked if it was recorded correctly (spelling, etc.). I responded without relating that I had relinquished the child, which they obviously had not yet learned. I informed them that the wrong man had been listed as the father and gave them the true father's name and description. I also corrected the information I had given at the hospital that I had been married. They responded by mail that those changes would not be made. A year or two later I wrote to the bureau, as the mother, requesting a copy of the birth certificate and enclosing a money order made out to the bureau. As expected, the reply was to return the money order and write, "Since this child has been legally adopted, we cannot furnish you the information requested".

Before finishing I should update you on Kim's natural father. He had occasionally called my mother in an effort to try to reach me. Although he and his family were aware of the pregnancy, he never mentioned this to her, at my direction. He continued to try to learn about me through her for several years. She never told him I had returned, but she did inform me whenever he called. In November of

1972, a mutual friend told me that he had been sent to prison. This was not hard to believe. I contacted him and visited him at the State Penitentiary. I told him about Kim. He was very surprised and unhappy. He could not believe that she was completely gone. As of this writing I have recently learned that he was shot by another prisoner and killed. He had only a mother and sister who cared about him.

My conclusion regarding Kim's adoption has been of uncertainty, but I have pretty consistently believed that she is fortunate I relinquished her. It would take an exceptional single parent to provide the time and contacts she probably enjoys in her adoptive family. Probably her extended adoptive family is more accepting of her racial background than mine might be. I regret that she cannot know some of the warmth and "soul" of her natural paternal family. Both of her natural grandmothers have shed tears over her absence and treasure their picture of her as a newborn. I know her paternal grandmother meant it deeply when she said "Barbara, I would have taken care of her for you if you would have brought her home". Yes, I'm sure I knew that even then and I must have made the decision I did only because of deep depression and lack of personal support.

I want to be happy that Kim has a good, normal, full family. But I also want to share a little bit of her too. I have resigned myself to the fact that we will not know her as a child. But I want so much to know about her. I would be sick to think that I ever interfered in her upbringing or upset or frightened her family. I feel very warmly toward them and much gratitude.

There seems to be no basic answer to this largely because so few people seem to accept that this is all there is to it. Knowing how many others share this burden and how much more difficult it usually is than is expressed, has helped. Perhaps being from a small family where each individual means so much and the fact that I have no other children has made things harder. This child has really been the central concern of my life for the years since her birth and I know this will remain so. I need to concentrate more personal efforts on things I can effect positively. I remind myself how fortunate I am to have Sister Diane to keep me informed of Kim's progress and that she has found a home so much better than many.

Jeanne — Age 37 (married the birthfather)

What I am about to reveal was, for a large part of my life, a deep, dark forbidden secret. It was something I was supposed to forget about completely — at least from the assumptions of those around me.

At a time in my life when I was the most vulnerable, those closest to me tried to convince me to give up my first born child — a child who was conceived in love and has been loved ever since by both her birthfather and myself. They succeeded in forcing me to give her up physically, but never emotionally.

I was 16 when I conceived my baby and 17 when she was born. Her father, who was 20 when she was born, wanted to marry me, but was unable at the time to get a divorce.

I never had given any thought to giving my baby up for adoption. I was never told that I could put the baby in a foster home until I got on my feet. No positive solution was ever offered to me — only adoption. My doctor said he knew a couple who could not have children and who could provide my child with more than I could ever dream of doing. This statement, among others, contributed to my already guilty feelings surrounding my pregnancy.

He proceeded to paint a glowing picture of the adoptive parents, while simultaneously pointing out to me all of my liabilities and emphasizing the fact that I would be able to have other children as I was perfectly healthy. I never agreed to the adoption even then because in my heart I was hoping that something could be worked out. In fact, I ran away twice to try to convince my mother and step-father of my need to keep this baby. These attempts were futile and only contributed to my negative feelings about myself.

My daughter was born on a Saturday morning at 6:45. When I

asked to see the baby, I was told by the nurse that she would bring her to me shortly. When my mother and doctor came in to see me, I told them that the nurse was going to bring the baby in to see me. With that, the doctor quickly made arrangements to have me taken off the maternity floor. I was whisked up to the next floor, put into a private room and given a tranquilizer.

Whenever I asked about the baby, I was told that she was just fine and that I would see her as soon as I was well enough to go downstairs. The only company I had was my mother and stepfather. They would only stay for short periods because I would start to cry; they would tell me that it would all be over soon and that I would forget and then they would leave.

When the baby's father came in to see me, he was told to leave the hospital or they would have him arrested. I became hysterical and within minutes a nurse came in and gave me an injection to quiet me down. Shortly after that, my parents and the lawyer for the adoptive couple had arrived. I told them that I wasn't going to sign anything and my mother told me that this paper was merely a formality and was not a surrender paper.

When I questioned a few things on the paper, I was reprimanded for doing so and by this time the tranquilizer had begun to take effect. I had neither the emotional nor the physical strength at that point. The nurse literally picked up my hand and signed my name.

I had been told during this confrontation that I would be permitted to dress her. This proved to be a lie. I was helped into a wheelchair and brought down to the nursery. There the nurse handed me a fully dressed bundle. When I tried to get her little hand out to look at it, she started to cry and so did I. The lawyer then told me to give the baby to the nurse and my mother informed me that the adoptive parents were waiting outside.

I never signed any other papers than the one I was forced to sign in the hospital. I always thought I would be able to have my baby back. During the next year, the father and I married. We began to plan for the future which included our child. A short time after we married we received a notice that the adoption finalization was to take place. My mother went with us and testified that I had been forced to sign the papers. The judge said she would take everything under advisement and we would be notified of her decision. Ten days later we received notice that she had decided the baby would be better off with the present family.

I cannot describe my feelings. To me it was a legal kidnapping that has lasted 18 years. Years in which I didn't know if she was dead

94

or alive; happy or unhappy. I didn't know if perhaps her new parents had died and left her an orphan. You cannot imagine the feeling of giving birth to a child and then never knowing what happens to that child.

Since I had no money, there wasn't anything I could do. I came to terms with the whole situation by dreaming of a reunion with my child. I always knew that one would take place. She was 16½ when she persuaded her adoptive parents to assist her in finding us. It was quite easy for them to do since the same lawyer who handled the adoption was a business associate of her adoptive father.

The reunion went beautifully. She agreed to have an ongoing relationship with us and was looking forward to meeting her brother and sister. Within a few days we received a phone call from her telling us that she had changed her mind. This is how our relationship now stands.

Though we do not have an ongoing relationship at the present time, I would like to say that knowing about her is a thousand times better than not knowing. I am glad that we had the opportunity to meet – if only once – if only briefly.

Section III – Education and Legislation

*"Adoption needs a new definition and a new structure. The require-
ment to see adoption as the same as a natural family should be
abandoned. The guilts of adoptive parents could be relieved by the
simple process of presenting adoption as a way that all of the parents
of the child are co-operating to plan for the future of a child. This
requires acknowledgement of the natural mother as an interested
party – and it is right that she should be considered. To re-structure
adoption as a form of marriage makes the relationship valid, provides
the freedom to acknowledge true feelings and enhances the possibilities
for a stronger relationship than the current adoption structure can
guarantee. No really good relationship is built on feelings of guilt,
exploitation, avoidance of reality and deceit."*

– Margaret Lawrence, in a paper
"Inside, Looking Out – of Adoption"
presented in the APA Symposium
in Washington, 1976.

Social Background of Adoption Laws

In the first half of the nineteenth century, it became apparent that public means for the care of dependent children were grossly inadequate for the welfare of the children. At first the system of private care was like the old methods of public care, with an initial period where the children were kept in an asylum or institution to receive rudimentary education, followed by indenture or apprenticeship.

It was soon apparent that the old systems were failing to educate and provide for the needs of the children because of changing economic conditions, and through the efforts of philanthropists, private agencies were formed for the care of dependent children.

As it became impossible to provide early institutional care for all, private agencies began to channel their energies toward placing children, often at very early ages, in foster homes where they would be treated more like members of the family than like servants. Motivating many, if not all, of the child-welfare reformers was a strong religious spirit which was an offshoot of a religious revival then taking place. The reformers believed that the children of the poor were not basically different from the children of the rich. The religious views of many of the child welfare workers led them to abandon the system of apprenticeship and to conclude that the best way for caring for dependent children was to have them accepted into "God's Reformatory", a family. Since a child who was not indentured could not be bound to a family in which he was not properly cared for, the effort to provide a proper family became paramount.

Many of the children placed by such agencies as the Children's

Aid Society found themselves in situations which not only resembled "adoption" as we know it today, but which was called by the same name.

As the phenomenon of children in adopted homes became more common, there was increased pressure not only to pass laws regulating and insuring the legal relations between adopted children and their natural and adoptive parents, but to guarantee that some benefits of heirship were conferred on the adopted child. This pressure, which originated with the activities of the charitable associations working in child welfare, led to the passage of the general adoption statutes in the third quarter of the nineteenth century.

The legally sanctioned custom of adopting children as heirs was unknown to the common law, although it was well-known in Roman practice, and passed nearly unchanged in the civil law. No general adoption statutes were passed in America before about 1850; no British statute was enacted before 1926. Once American legislatures had begun to act on the problem of adoption, however, it was not long before a host of states enacted some form of adoption law. Within 25 years of the passage of the first statutes, 24 states had adoption legislation.

The most advanced early law on adoption which we have is from the Romans. The Roman law which was bound up in the Roman concept of "parental power" explains their notion that one can have a connection with one family only. In its original form that meant complete power over the offspring, including the power of life and death. This aspect of the Roman law had a strong effect on American judges, who were repelled by Roman parental power since *"with us, every man who has reached his majority is free from anyone else's power"*.

The first comprehensive adoptive statute was passed in 1851 in Massachusetts. Among its key provisions were requirements that written consent be given by the natural parents of the child to be adopted; that the child himself must consent if he was fourteen years of age or older; that the adoptor's wife or husband must join in the petition for adoption; that the probate judge to whom the petition for adoption was presented must be satisfied that the petitioners were "of sufficient ability to bring up the child...and that it is fit and proper that such adoption should take effect" before he could decree and confirm the adoption; that once the adoption was approved by the probate court, the adopted child would become "to all intents and purposes" the legal child of the petitioners; that the natural parents would be deprived by the decree of adoption of all legal rights and obligations respecting the adopted child; and that any petitioner or child who is the subject of such a petition might appeal to the Supreme Judicial Court from the decree of the probate judge.

Most of the adoption statutes were directly copied from the Massachusetts law. The "avowed object" of the Massachusetts law was that of "securing to adopted children a proper share in the estate of adopting parents who die intestate". William H. Whitmore, who wrote the treatise "The Law of Adoption (1876)" viewed many of the features of the adoption statutes with alarm. He had originally written his treatise "for the purpose of assisting a committee of the Massachusetts legislature in considering the questions of a proposed change in the laws of that state." He noted that the law was "unnecessarily and unwisely broad in its terms". Whitmore was puzzled by the fact that most of the statutes made no provision regarding the duration of the relation that was to be created between adopted parents and children. Whitmore saw the purpose of the law as protecting adopted children during their minority should their adopted parents die or somehow neglect to provide for them in their wills. He then suggested that adoption be only a temporary relationship, extending perhaps throughout the period of the child's minority, with a "reasonable provision" provided upon setting him out in the world at his majority. Whitmore finished his evaluation with the observation that guidelines needed to be set up to insure that a child adopted in one state would be treated equitably in all. He summed up his views "Evidently as the matter stands, the attempts of philanthropists to cure a small evil may have resulted in a serious injury to the rights of many other persons." Today in 1979, we could add our "Amen" to that statement written some 103 years ago.

For a more in-depth study, read *The Historical Background of the American Law of Adoption* by Stephen B. Presser in the *Journal of Family Law*, Vol. II, 1971.

Our Hypocritical Society

There are many in the adoption triangle who feel that abortion is an even better solution to the teenage pregnancy epidemic than adoption. While I do not believe in the adoption process as it is presently constituted, I cannot in good conscience condone abortion. In adoption we speak of the adoptees rights taking precedent over those of the birthparent, and I believe they do. What about the "rights" of the unborn child over those who chose to conceive (even though accidentally).

We are a schizophrenic society. As stated by Dr. C. Everett Koop in his book entitled "The Right To Live, The Right To Die", he makes the following comparison: "We will fly a deformed newborn baby four hundred miles by airplane to perform a series of remarkable operations knowing full well that the end result will be far less than perfect. We will ship food to a starving nation overseas, and at the same time, supply arms to its enemy. We will feed another starving people beset by famine, but we will make no attempt to ask them to try to control their population by contraception. We will stop a cholera epidemic by vaccine in a country unable to feed itself, so that the people can survive cholera in order to die of starvation. While we struggle to save the life of a three-pound baby in a hospital's newborn intensive care unit, obstetricians in the same hospital are destroying similar infants yet unborn."

The modern practice of abortion first appeared as a policy of government in the communist dictatorships, where contempt for the dignity of human life is widely demonstrated.

You may wonder why I'm concerning myself about abortion while writing a story about adoption. The reason is this: alternatives

103

to the present adoption system are needed. It is obvious that the present system is not being appropriated since most girls today choose to either keep their babies or have an abortion.

We are all aware that our nation was founded on the principles of human rights — the right to *life*, liberty, and the pursuit of happiness. One by one these things are being taken from us. The Supreme Court ruled only five years ago that an unborn *child* in the womb is not a person entitled to the right to life. Where has our sanctity for life gone? We've become indifferent. I realized in looking back over my own experience that I could have spared myself a lot of hurt if I had had an abortion.

What have we as a society come to when we punish the woman who chooses to give life — regardless of her marital status — and by the same token we urge her to abort (killing a child while still in the womb). I applaud anyone today who chooses to face whatever need be in order to give forth life. This will illustrate my point.

Recently there was an article in the newspaper about a woman who was demoted in her job because she became pregnant out of wedlock. No one would have given it a second thought had she chosen abortion, but because she chose to have her child, she was being punished for it — punished for giving life!

It really is unfortunate that each year more than a million unborn babies are executed whose only crime is being unwanted. A murderer receives due process of the law. He is given legal counsel to defend his rights and witnesses to testify on his behalf. A jury of twelve hears and weighs the evidence bearing on his guilt or innocence. If only one member of the jury has a reasonable doubt, his life is spared. The unborn child (like the adoptee) has no defense, no legal counsel. Society does not even give the unborn the benefit of the doubt. The reason our forefathers enacted laws permitting capital punishment was due to their high regard for human life. How far we've come from their original thinking!

Isn't it possible that if we "loosened up" on the adoption laws and made them more humane for the birthparents that maybe they would choose adoption over abortion. Do young girls today feel abortion is an easier solution for them than to give up a child that they may never see again? Maybe we will have to consider this if we are going to turn the tide. Certainly we need to reconsider the whole adoption process if the institution is going to survive in today's society. What can we do to improve the system?

Improving the System

It's only been since the latter 40s that laws have been passed in most states that require information about birthparents be kept confidential. At the present time there are only a few states that do not have such a law. Alabama and Kansas have open records. In Pennsylvania, the legally emancipated adult adoptee may have access to his original birth certificate simply by requesting it from the Department of Vital Statistics. However, this law is in conflict with the adoption law which requires records to be sealed. Legislators are now working avidly to bring these two laws into alignment − in favor of confidentiality! In Ohio an adult adoptee may have identifying information about the original parents if they appear in person at the courthouse and prove their identity. In Scotland, Finland and Israel, they may also have access to the original birth certificate by producing evidence about themselves. England and Wales have recently passed a law giving access to the original certificate providing the adoptee agrees to an interview with an adoption counselor.

The time has surely come when we need to study and clarify the various controversial issues and to provide some sort of guidelines to establish future adoption policy. Many adoption activist groups have been formed to serve that very purpose. Several individuals and groups all across the U.S. are petitioning the courts to test the constitutional legality of keeping the adoptee's records sealed for life. It's a sad commentary that this is even necessary since the sealed record is an absolute assault upon human freedom; a freedom which everyone else in our country can exercise except the adoptee. The freedom to ask for and receive an original birth certificate. Because of this lack of freedom, adoption in our country continues to be propagated on the basis of a LIE.

Certainly the role of the birthparent following the culmination of the adoption proceeding needs to be considered, which up until now has been neglected. There should be a more direct involvement with the adoptive parents — possibly allowing the birth and adoptive parents to meet one another at the time of the adoption, thereby giving both sets of parents a better position of reality, as suggested by Sorosky, Panner and Baran in their book *The Adoption Triangle*. This would eliminate the need for either to have to resort to denial that the other exists or projection in order to deal with the whole proceeding. The adoptive parents should be provided with continuing updated reports about the birthparent in order to answer their child's inevitable questions. That would certainly minimize the chances of the adoptee resorting to fantasizing in an attempt to fill the need for identity. Information could also be made available to the birthparents about their child's progress and development which would help to lessen the pain of having to relinquish one's own flesh and blood.

Open Adoption

An "Open Adoption" would be that adoption in which the birthparents meet the adoptive parents, participate in the separation and placement process, relinquish all legal, moral and nurturing rights, *but* retain the right to knowledge of the child's whereabouts and welfare. This arrangement would most likely free a number of children available for adoption in those cases where the birthparents are unwilling to cut ties to the child. People question over and over again why children are kept in foster care and why the mother won't give them up. The unwillingness to "let go" for a lifetime certainly appears to be the logical answer.

If adoption is going to continue to flourish in the American system, we are going to have to cut through the tape which seals records and give more consideration to the one who gave the child life in the first place. With abortion being an easy way out today, a girl or woman carrying a child out of wedlock needs to be commended and recognized as a person in her own right with needs and feelings. Up until recently the unwed mother was shuffled out of town, sent to a maternity home, away from the peering eyes of society in order to cover up the terrible sin she had committed. The guilt trip which was placed upon her, in many instances, carried throughout the rest of her life. Birthparents as a whole have suffered from the inhumanity of the social service agencies because they were poor, helpless, and young. Because they had no advocate to speak on their behalf, they were treated as though they had done a terrible thing by having a child.

What can be done to redress the wrongs that have been done — who have been the victims of these kinds of services — the parents who have lost their children and the children who have lost their "roots"? John L. Brown, Editor of *Family Involvement Magazine*, has stated that "In all of man's inhumanity to man throughout the history of mankind, those deeds which are done in anger and hostility can be redressed and dealt with by the victims and by society at large because you can fight against evil, you can fight against wrongs and you can get support in that fight; but the inhumanity that is done in the name of 'good', in the name of 'help', in the name of 'service' — that is the kind of inhumanity that offers no opportunity for redress. To attack the do-gooders is to alienate yourself and to fight against the system is to fight against 'good' structure; it's to fight against those parts of society that are supposed to be caring for the needs of people, and so the victims are victims without recourse, with no opportunity for obtaining sympathetic support. What we see in the laws that have effected the life of children is that if a child had a need that extended beyond his family's capacity to cope with it, the system robbed these children and their parents of the right to redress the wrongs that were done in the name of 'service'."

Mr. Brown suggests that each person take a stand — that there is no place in this important issue for middle-grounders or moderates. You are either for or against a system that wrongs people. If no other action or outlet seems appropriate for you, then the one thing you can do is to join or support adoption activists groups such as Orphan Voyage, Alma, or CUB.

It is time for us to realize that openness and honesty must replace the secrecy and anonymity that have prevailed in adoption. For the millions of people whose lives are touched by adoption and who are still in pain, we should work to develop firmer resolutions that will meet both past and future needs.

The immediate changes that need to be made are: The opening of the original birth records to adult adoptees upon request; counseling services on a continuing basis should be provided through the agencies since adoption itself is an ongoing process which never stops; alternatives need to be considered in order to provide homes for those children who would not otherwise be cared for; and most importantly, medical information should be placed in the file at the time of birth and then on a regular basis. Medical problems do arise in subsequent years and this way the adoptive family could be kept informed.

A central registry is being maintained so that birthparents and adult adoptees may enter their desire for reunion on a voluntary basis. Should both parties register, their meeting could be more easily facilitated. Emma Villardi of Carson City, Nevada, who is interested in genealogy has set up this national registry in the United States. Anyone desiring more information and/or a registration form should contact her directly. Include a self-addressed stamped envelope. She charges no fee for this service!

There is a definite need for some sort of legal counsel for the unwed mother. When one considers that an underage birthparent cannot vote, drive, be drafted, or sign any legal documents, it seems absurd that we would ask that same birthparent to sign a document giving away her own flesh and blood. Birthparents are often under severe stress when they sign the relinquishment papers and by the time they realize the full force of their action, it is too late. Social workers and/or family members are known to use tremendous psychological pressure towards adoption and offer no alternative plan to help her keep the child. Whatever happened to the extended family concept? I am convinced that many of our black families have been instituting "open adoption" for years by having a sister, an aunt, or close friend, step in and be a surrogate mother for whatever time was needed.

In conclusion, following is a ten-point program proposed for transition to Open Adoption as suggested by Jean Paton, who is the Director of Orphan Voyage in Cedaredge, Colorado. Jean was a pioneer of the movement back in the early 50s when the rest of us thought "roots" belonged only to trees.

1) Open records to persons adopted before records went under seal, and to their natural parents, giving notification of this.

2) Open records to adoptees who are 25 years of age or older.

3) Open records to adoptees between 18 and 25 years of age whose adoptive parents state the matter has been covered and discussed and who wish to cooperate.

4) Appoint and provision a Monitoring group to supervise the above and to arrive at an agreed upon plan for people who are under the age of 18 and those not covered in point 3.

5) New adoptions will clearly indicate to all parties that records will be available to all parties at least by the time the adoptee reaches maturity.

6) To provide for preparation for open records, there should be education. It should not be expected that the young adult adoptee reaches maturity ready for contact with his natural parents if they have never been presented to him before that time. Each adoption should be accompanied by full information about the original parents, and there should be some way of insuring that this information is conveyed to the adopted person.

7) Natural parents should receive follow-up information about the well-being of their children surrendered to adoption, and should be encouraged to anticipate future reconciliation.

8) The State should provide financial assistance for a Reunion File, for use in difficult cases; and for an indigenous group to service problems arising from the sealed record and the transition to an open system of adoption.

9) The State should be alert to the three-party movement now taking place within the population of adoption, and that this movement will increasingly seek effective influence on adoption policies and practices. Ultimately the best help comes from those who have experienced this very different form of family life.

10) Educate for openness, and toward the undoing of destructive attitudes brought about by misunderstandings and misuse of the sealed record provisions in adoption law.

Adoption Education

According to Webster, ignorance implies a lack of knowledge either generally or on one particular subject. It is not necessarily one's own fault as it is usually due to lack of exposure. It becomes one's fault when one hears the facts presented and chooses to disregard them deliberately or refuses to consider the facts given. Because of the compounded issues involved in adoption and because the emotions surrounding it run deep, this is so often the case.

How then is education concerning the changes in adoption going to come about? For years just the mention of the word adoption caused everyone to speak a little softer — it carried an aura as though at its mere mention, a huge skeleton would come forth.

Today in 1979 those involved in the adoption triangle have chosen to unveil themselves — to step out of the shadows and expose the many wrongs that have been done in the name of "adoption". That is not to say there are no rights about the system, but only that there needs to be change before it can truly be considered a humane institution.

The education will mainly come through the adoption activist groups that are cropping up all over the country at a rate too fast to keep up with (see list in appendix). This is where most of the education has come from to date — from the people directly involved — from the self-help groups — from those who have personally experienced inner turmoil, frustration, and anxiety.

I am going to zero in on one particular group since this group has met my particular need and since it covers the main subject of this book — that of the birthparents who have surrendered their children to adoption. The group is called Concerned United Birthparents, Inc.

111

(C.U.B.). In July of 1976, four young women met at a church in southeast Massachusetts to discuss their experiences of surrendering a child. Lee Campbell, organizer of that first meeting, began the work of contacting other birthparents that were known to her through her involvement in an adoptee activist group and through readers of a Boston newspaper letter column. The incorporation of the non-profit group was effected in October of 1976. In April of 1977, yours truly invited Lee to speak at the first annual conference of the Adoption Forum of Philadelphia, of which I was an active Board Member. The Adoption Forum consists of all three parts of the triangle and is interested in opening the lines of communication between each with an emphasis toward more mutual respect.

At that time Lee and I had an opportunity to spend a few hours together discussing her hopes and dreams for C.U.B. with a little input from me. I volunteered to start a satellite group of C.U.B. which would cover eastern Pennsylvania and southern New Jersey. That became the first branch, which I formed in July 1977, and am presently coordinating. In less than a year we had become a self-supporting branch with some 50 members.

I'm sure that as Lee and I sat that evening in the Philadelphia airport and discussed the varying aspects of adoption, we never dreamed that it would mushroom in the short time that it has.

With C.U.B. being less than three years old, we are now sixteen branches strong with requests coming in from all over the country to begin new ones. The loud cry from those in power that "birthparents need and want protection" is fast becoming only a soft whimper. We have united our voices to answer some of the following questions:

What is Concerned United Birthparents, Inc.?

Concerned United Birthparents, Inc. (CUB) is an autonomous national non-profit support and advocacy group for parents who have surrendered children for adoption. We also have a strong interest and concern with teen pregnancy prevention, and with informed-choice availability in all untimely pregnancies. In addition to being a resource group for studies being conducted on the aftermath of adoption, we also constitute the only nationally organized group available for those who research the dynamics of teen pregnancies and untimely pregnancies in adults. CUB is not a search organization; any searches conducted by our members are personal ventures.

112

The term used by agencies and professionals refers to the "relinquishment" of a child. Yet you use the term "surrender". Why?

"Surrender" fits the experience. Because the child is "given up" without options, often under pressure tactics, and because there is no emotional compensation for the loss, there is a real "surrender". When options are available to the birthparent in the adoption process, then we would like to see the term "placed" used. No child should ever have to think he was given away, and no mother should ever have to live with the guilt of giving away a child.

Why do you use the term "birthparents" instead of the many other terms used?

We find the terms "biological" and "bio-parent" descriptive of a mechanical incubator or unfeeling human baby machine. We are neither; our continued love and concern for our birthchildren is akin to any parents' for their children. Although we do not object to the term "natural parent", we find many adoptive parents rightly resent the implication that they are "unnatural" parents, for they may parent quite naturally, indeed. Therefore, we choose the term "birthparent", one word, anologous to terms like "grandparent", "grandmother", or "grandfather". We remain the child's progenitor and thus find the term "birthparent" both accurate and sensitive to our place in the child's existence.

What is it that CUB really wants... isn't it to regain custody of the children?

Most emphatically, no! Most birthparents have gone on in life to create (and sometimes adopt) and raise other children. In this context, we know full well the commitment and sacrifices which go into proper parenting. For the adoptive parents' efforts, for their love, for the reality and integrity of their relationship with the child, most of us have only the highest respect and esteem. Moreover, we do not seek to assuage our own suffering by creating a situation which would threaten the psychological continuity of our birthchildren's parenting. Rather we seek to dimensionalize this sense of continuity by providing our children with a link to their birth history and knowledge of their own genetic future.

113

We also hope to illuminate and gain credence for the behind-the-scenes sacrifices we, too, have made for the child and the resultant ongoing pain of never knowing about the child, his/her parents, and how they all fare as life progresses. Most birthparents do not know whether the child is alive or dead. Certainly one of the most difficult challenges CUB faces is to finally present a true image of the birthparent who, because of the imposed secrecy in adoption, has long been enshrouded in mystery.

But it's true, isn't it, that some adoptive parents view CUB as a threat?

It is true that some adoptive parents consider birthparents as threats to their family. Some have organized to thwart both our efforts and the efforts of adoptees to obtain information. Previous research conducted on a personal level through a Boston newspaper revealed that there may be an equal number of adoptive parents, albeit less vocal, who, in varying degrees, are more receptive to expanding present adoption policies. In the March 1978 issue of CUB's newsletter, *The Communicator*, excerpts of many letters received from adoptive parents were printed. These people revealed their affection for, concern about, and desire to share information with "their" birthparents. We hope that time, communication, and public exposure of the true image of the birthparent will help to dispel the fears some adoptive parents have.

How has the social work profession reacted to CUB?

In this sector, too, we have found some who consider us threats. We seem to threaten the conventional wisdom on which many have built their professional careers. Other social workers, however, respond eagerly and view the newly exposed adoption problems as a chance to grow professionally. CUB very much wants to work with adoption professionals in creating loving, humane solutions.

What is CUB's position on the current controversy about adoptees' rights?

Adoptees have the absolute right to full and accurate information about their origins, including identification of, and meeting with, the birthparents, *whenever* and *whatever age there is a need*. During the child's minority years, we would like to see the adoptive parents use the agency as a conduit of information channeled by consenting birthparents. If all parties involved want a more personal exchange, of course this should be permitted, too.

When adoptees reach the age of 18, they are entitled to all information regardless of others' consent. They are entitled to the same respect and freedom of non-adopted adults, to the same knowledge of their birth history and birthparents as do non-adopted adults. We believe this supersedes an unwilling birthparents' right to anonymity. With this right, however, comes an inherent responsibility: adoptees should respect any need for discretion on their birthparents' part. Also, they should remain in communication with the birthparents following contact until healing of any re-opened wounds has taken place. It should be understood that any continuing relationship with the birthparent can only be the result of mutual desire.

What percentage of birthparents really do want anonymity?

Our experience — and researchers and activist groups who effect reunions agree — shows that only a scant minority want anonymity. The percentage of birthparents who want anonymity ranges from 5 to 18 percent. Most birthparents are overjoyed to finally know the fate of their birthchild, and to close a long, painful chapter of wondering. Dr. Arthur Sorosky, a California researcher, has described a birthparent's pain as a "sense of psychological amputation". Another researcher, Dr. Henry Grunebaum of Massachusetts, parallels the pain with that of the families of soldiers missing in action.

Birthparents oftentimes summarize the reunion experience as a re-establishment of themselves as "whole, complete" persons; feelings of "peace" prevail. From a legal point of view, CUB feels the closed record is an affront to the basic dignity extended other citizens: the right to take charge of our own affairs. The closed record perpetuates the assumption that birthparents have sinned, that we should feel guilty, and thus be "protected" from exposure to the "sin". The closed record implies that we are incapable of protecting ourselves as do other citizens. It implies that we are incapable of emotional depth, of accepting a new situation, and coping and growing with it. The closed record limits birthparents socially, imprisons us emotionally, and discriminates against us morally.

Do you think birthparents have the right to identifying information, too?

To never know your birthchild is to spend a lifetime in the anguish of forever wondering, a punishment disproportionate to the "crime" of giving birth and allowing another to parent the child. Birthparents should have the right to offer their hands in friendship, just as anyone else can.

Moreover, when birthparents initiate the reunion, it may help to take the "sting" out of the initial "rejection" that all adoptees either consciously, or unconsciously, feel about having been surrendered for adoption. Such contact by the birthparents can have great restorative and healing powers for the adopted. Additionally, though it is true that most birthparents welcome contact, adoptees nonetheless worry that their own birthparents may be among the minority who would not be welcoming; they may anxiously fantasize a second "rejection" needlessly. Hence, contact by the birthparents would erase this worry. Yes, we do indeed feel that birthparents should have the right to identifying information when the adoptee reaches age 18 — and before then, if the other parents agree. Just as is the case when the adoptee initiates contact, it would be understood that the formation of any kind of relationship is contingent on mutual desire.

What are the obstacles impeding adoption relationships?

In addition to restrictive laws, there is the prevailing social attitude. Curiosity about one's birthparents or birthchildren is seen as an unnatural and unhealthy thing. And, though many believe otherwise, there is *still* a stigma attached to unwed parenthood which results in the continuing, sometimes unconscious, desire of society to punish an unwed mother. Skeptics who say this bias is no longer prevalent will be interested to learn that a 1977 poll by Yankelovich, Skelly and White revealed that 70 percent of those polled "disapproved" of having children without marriage. Another impediment is the stereotype of birthparents as neurotic child-snatchers.

Therefore, people must not only be educated to accept the naturalness of adoption triangle members wanting to know each other, but they must strive to erase hidden prejudices and uprighteous punitive measures. Society must see that, in reality, birthparents bode no harm to those who know them. Moreover, people must expand the scope of their vision to see that curiosity and interest in one's lineage — be it past or future — speaks well of a healthy, inquisitive mind which, in any other circumstance, would bring enthusiastic endorsement from an approving community.

Many of CUB's members must have been pregnant teenagers. Do you have a solution for the so-called teenage pregnancy epidemic?

We share society's concern for the more than one million teenagers who become pregnant every year. We know that no matter which option they choose, it will have lifelong repercussions for them.

We believe the most effective solution is the prevention of teenage pregnancies. To this end, we endorse sex education in the schools: not only biological information, which should be introduced in the primary grades, but an expansion to include human relationships and personal development which should be incorporated in the secondary grades. This should delve into a wide range of social areas while exploring personal attitudes. Students should invite "been there" speakers, read personal anthologies. And then, to broaden their concept of personal impact, follow-up should take the form of projection into these roles and hypothesizing reactions and solutions to them. With this would come a higher order of morality in the most humanely valuable sense of the word.

We believe, too, that birth control should be readily and unconditionally available. We believe that once sex ceases to be a "dirty" word (so that one's participation need not be excused by feigning spontaniety), teenagers may "prepare" and assume control and responsibility for their actions should they enter into a sexual relationship.

Mentioned earlier was the need for informed choice in unplanned pregnancies. What do you mean by that?

Should an unplanned pregnancy develop, decisions about the pregnancy should evolve from theory to reality in less of a crisis atmosphere. An in-depth exploration of all the options available would be the first step in ensuring "informed choice". To wit, all school, pregnancy, and adoption counsellors as well as obstetrical clinics should be required by law to distribute to their clients a

117

WRITTEN report detailing the available options and their known lifetime repercussions, if any. The counsellors and clinic personnel should encourage their clients to give a copy of the report to the partner, the partner's family, and their own family. Additionally, if the pregnant individual is a student, a conference should be set up between teachers and community professionals to devise a course in pregnancy and parenting study from programs available both within the school and within the community.

Do you think teenagers should keep their babies?

Ideally, yes. This ideal situation would, of course, require a supportive home situation, a certain amount of maturity on the part of the teen, as well as a strong commitment to parenting by her; also needed is the identification and implementation of whatever assistance programs may be available.

According to Planned Parenthood's Report, "Eleven Million Teenagers", 87 percent of unmarried teen mothers do keep their babies nowadays despite disapproval from some people. This disapproval stems in part from the widely held assumption that teen moms are abusive to their children or neglectful, leaving children in extended foster care.

Our research, however, refutes these assumptions. A study by the Denver Research Association, "National Analysis of Official Child Neglect and Abuse Reporting", revealed that the *smallest* group of neglectful and abusive parents is those under 19; and this when many of these children are in day care where abuses are more likely to be detected and reported. The actual median age for the abusive parent is age 34!

Relative to extended foster care, the May 1977 NYC Comptroller's Report on Foster Care placed the blame on agency personnel who "too often failed to provide (birth) parents with needed services on a timely basis although they were found to be adequately staffed and reimbursed."

There are some social programs (a particularly effective post-natal program located in Boston) but these resources may go untapped due to agency neglect in revealing their availability. Therefore, we strongly reiterate the need for all options to be presented to those experiencing untimely pregnancies in *writing*.

The problem then is that many agency personnel have incorporated the prejudices of society against teen and single parenthood and need to re-evaluate personal attitudes and agency commitment to rectify this situation.

What about adoption then? Is CUB against adoption?

CUB cannot endorse the *present system* of adoption. Apparently, neither can the pregnant-out-of-wedlock teen today, for only 8 percent choose adoption (about 5 percent send the child to live with relatives or friends). We who have surrendered under the present system understand all too well the reason why pregnants today, who can see the disadvantages to themselves and to their children that adoption offer, eschew adoption.

Nevertheless, CUB believes that adoption could be considered an alternative in some cases. It would have to be a different, more expansive kind of adoption. We suggest "Round Table Adoption" (ROTA). This should not be confused with "open adoption" which encompasses visitation rights, for with ROTA, some persons may not wish to choose visitation rights for themselves although this would be an option for consideration. ROTA allows freedom of choice for both the birthparents *and* the adoptive parents, with an agency or adoption lawyer mediating in the working out of a plan amenable to both parties. We envision it working like this:

If the birthparents-to-be wanted to explore the possibilities of adoption, they should be guided in exploring and projecting their individual needs in adoption until they are mutually agreeable. Then, they should feel free to "adoption-shop" among adoption workers and adoption lawyers. There they would peruse background information on a small, agency-selected group of ten or so prospective adoptive families who had projected their needs to be compatible with the birthparents' own, who had successfully completed agency screening, and, if applicable, infertility counseling.

This would all be considered food-for-thought as the pregnancy progressed.

After the birth, if adoption was still considered a possibility, a lawyer would be made available to the new parents. A rough draft of an adoption plan would be drawn up based upon review of the birthparents' needs. This adoption plan would be mediated with the chosen adoptive couple and ideally with a guardian ad-litem educated in this area who would represent the child's best interest. Assuming all were agreeable and comfortable with the plan, three weeks or more after the birth of the child, the adoption plan would be formalized and

119

legalized.

This type of client-centered adoption wherein all participants come together in reality and respect for each other's roles would contain certain non-negotiable rights.

1. The adoption plan would be irrevocable so long as the terms were upheld: to wit, if the child is later "returned" or if the adoptive parents pre-decease the minor child without competent guardianship provided for the child. In those cases, the birthparent would be notified, be considered as a potential parent, or become involved in renegotiating a new adoption plan.

2. The birthparents would be notified when the adoption's interlocutory degree was finalized. Also, if the child pre-deceases the birthparents, the birthparents would be notified.

3. All medical information and requests for medical information would be promptly forwarded to the other parties.

4. The need for anonymity during the child's minority years, if contracted, may decrease with either set of parents as security and maturity take root. Hence, any party may later relinquish their right to anonymity and notification of same would be conveyed to the other parties. A renegotiation of this aspect would then be considered IF the other parties were agreeable.

5. When the adopted individual becomes 18 years of age, ALL contracted anonymity would become null and void.

6. The original birth certificate would be available to the birthparents.

Then, there would be the negotiable rights. It is important to say here that the sampling below is merely food-for-thought. Uppermost is CUB's belief that the adoption plan should reflect the needs of the principals involved: *never* that of any organization, any agency, or any other person.

- birthparent participation in the selection process of adoptive parents
- complete anonymity on both sides (closed adoption) until the

120

child reaches age 18 with the understanding #4 above could later be invoked
- no restrictions regarding anonymity on either side
- pre-adoption meeting of both sets of parents
- ceremony to bind the adoption plan
- choosing the name together or retaining the birth name or relinquishing rights to name the child
- post-adoption meetings between parents
- visitation rights with a child at a certain age or immediately
- agreement to allow the child access to identifying information before age 18
- periodic reports, mutual or one-sided: maybe with pictures

This form of adoption is the only adoption CUB recognizes as responsible, viable, and life-consistent. With this form of adoption, birthparents would not labor under lifetime feelings of child abandonment for they would have actively participated in making responsible plans for that child's welfare. This form of adoption forces its participants to recognize the other's contribution to the child's life; there would be no fantasy, no pretense. Moreover, the children would have the security of *knowing* that their birthparents were not rejecting; that they were, and are, caring. Allowing birthparents responsible control over their child's destiny will manifest itself in positive ways throughout the remainder of the birthparents' lives; in educational and career pursuits, in future personal relationships, marriage, and subsequent children.

If the birthparents choose adoption, it should be recognized and held by all that the birthparents' love is as equal and abiding as any parent's.

(Taken from "The Birthparent Perspective" booklet © C.U.B. 1978.)

What are C.U.B.'s immediate goals and means of reaching them?

We expect to devise a questionnaire which will be distributed to agencies nationwide which will obtain the information we need to advise and refer people properly.

In an attempt to get others to recognize birthparents as people needy and worthy of social space, we will continue to submit to media coverage knowing full well the impact which good publicity brings.

Shortly we expect to have an "informed choice" booklet which would clearly state our sincerity that we believe each individual should make their own decision based upon the known facts. This booklet would be distributed to the parents-to-be who write us as well as to pregnancy clinics, schools, maternity shelters, bureau heads, and the like, for a nominal fee.

Adoption legislation will be introduced throughout the coming year. The "Consent to Inform" bill which was introduced in Massachusetts will be the main thrust of CUB's legislation reform.

What is the "Consent to Inform" bill all about?

Simply stated — the natural parent of a minor adopted child may at any time in writing to the agency who processed such adoption, consent to inform the adoptive parents, through the agency, of information desired by the adoptive parents. Upon receipt of a Consent to Inform, such agency would notify the adoptive parents that one has been received from the natural parents, and that the natural parent may disclose only information he/she desires to disclose. Such agency would then notify the adoptive parents. Thereafter, the adoptive parents may request such information through the agency and the agency would then contact the natural parent to provide such information.

What would this bill mean to adoptive parents?

Implementation of this legislation would provide adoptive parents with a much needed option; the option of choosing whether they would like to receive updated information when they request it on their child's biological history in order to satisfy their child's questions and curiosity, as these arise through his/her life.

If they choose affirmatively, they would be parenting on a basis of knowledge, and not assumption, of their child's heritage.

They would be aware of their child's physical capabilities and latent talents. They would have forewarning of hereditary diseases as they become known over time. It would solidify their relationship with the child by allowing them to provide the same answers that are available in non-adoptive familial relationships. They would have the peace of mind, and the joy of heart, to know they are providing, as completely as possible, every avenue for development in their child's life.

122

What would this bill mean to the adoptees?

Implementation of this bill will provide adoptees with the opportunity to receive these answers through the proper source (their adoptive parents), during their minority years. In this way, they will have the benefit of a more "normal" familial relationship whereby nuances of biological identity and history are available as they are in non-adoptive families. They will have access to genetic information. The bill will erase "unknowns" before they escalate into obsessions. Adoptees will have the opportunity to anticipate their physical development as well as have an awareness of their potential talents, thereby alleviating the "differences" between them and their non-adopted peers.

Chapter 785 of the Acts of 1972 of the Commonwealth of Massachusetts stresses the commitment of state government to assure every child "a fair and full opportunity to reach his full potential". This proposed legislation is entirely consistent with this goal.

What would this bill mean to Birthparents?

Implementation of this bill would bring peace — an end to the frustrating inability to provide information to help their birthchild. It would bring a special kind of joy — the knowledge of further contributing to their birthchild's happiness. For the birthchild's happiness is, and has always been, the main hope and prayer of a concerned birthparent.

Finally, the crux of the legislation is this: A birthparent who does not wish to be "protected" should not be required to be protected. A birthparent who is willing to provide information to benefit another, should have the opportunity to offer same. Adoptive parents should have the option to decide for themselves whether they wish to take advantage of this offer. It is, most importantly, a matter between adult individuals, and the decision should be afforded them in an individual and adult manner. The adoption agency should assume its rightful role of continuing intermediary in adoption, thus creating a humane approach to a system fast deteriorating because of its inhumanity.

And the Letters Pour In...

As Coordinator of the Concerned United Birthparents local chapter (Pa./S.Jersey), hundreds of letters have crossed my desk in the short time we have been in existence. To give you better insight of the various feelings surrounding adoption, I share the following letters with you.

It was ten years ago, at the age of 24, that I gave up my son for adoption. At that time, the boy's father was married, with four children of his own, so marriage with me was out of the question. I was horribly confused at that time, as I dearly loved both the baby and his father, but I had to think in terms of providing a family unit in a home where I knew he would be cared for as a member of a family. However, not one day since I gave him up for adoption has passed that I don't think of him with both pain and regret. It would be unbearable for me to think that when he becomes old enough to wonder why he was given up that he would think it was because he wasn't loved or wanted.

M.F., Pennsylvania

This letter from a birthparent expresses a decline in her life since giving up her child. Many have repeated what she has to say:

I am a desperate Mother who would give anything to be reunited with my 16-year-old daughter. I am married again with another child, but I would love to know that my child is alive and in a good home. I suffered a nervous breakdown after my baby was born. At the time the question of adoption came up, I had no money, no husband, and no

125

home of my own. My life has been the gradual deterioration of a smart, intelligent, fun-loving, happy girl into a nervous, depressed and sad woman. Please help me find my child.

S.H., California

This gal cannot remember the date that she relinquished, which is not unusual since many cannot even remember the date they gave birth. It has become a mental block for them:

Right now even though I have just begun to write, I feel as if someone is ripping my heart out. I suppose that everyone who has given up children for adoption must feel the same as I. I fear what they must think of me. I can remember that last time I saw my oldest daughter. She had on a dark blue dotted swiss dress — she looked so old for her few years. The look on her face will never be erased from my mind. She seemed to have an expression that said, "Why am I here?" I have often wondered if she knew what was happening. Like so many others, the day I signed those papers giving up my girls, I was told that it was better for all concerned. I asked if I might send birthday cards and such. I was told very clearly and in one word *NO*! I have lived that dreadful day over and over again. I cannot remember the date, but I will never forget the pain I felt then and now. I dare not hope that I would ever find them in my lifetime, but my husband and I would like to leave what little we have to them.

G.A., Florida

This comes from a 56-year-old adoptee after attending her first meeting of the adoption group:

I'm sure that I do not need to tell you the impact — the positive impact the organization has brought to my sense of well-being. In just two weeks time I have had the moral courage to begin my search and the support and understanding is beyond expression. Heretofore, I've been knocked down alone! As I gain momentum and balance, I will be, in any way possible, a strong proponent and effective supporter of your cause.

J. McM., Philadelphia

This birthmother relates guilt feelings that many of us carry for years:

126

I still feel guilty about giving my baby away — I was not married. I find now I am a stronger person — had it happened in my present frame of mind, knowing what I now know, things would have been different. I would like any information I can obtain. Maybe I'll feel better about myself — for I now feel that I deserted my child.

In response to a newspaper article about C.U.B., this birthparent wrote:

> As a birthparent myself who has kept this secret for seven years, along with the many questions that have run through my mind about my son, I found the article very comforting and would like to know more about your organization. Any person or group who can help a birthparent cope with her most precious secret and feelings should be commended and a simple thank you doesn't seem enough. Thank you in advance for anything you can offer me in learning to admit to and live with my secret.

G.A., Ohio

Regarding the next letter — many birthmothers marry the birth-father within a year or two after relinquishment, and go on to have other children which are the full siblings of the child put up for adoption.

> I am a birthparent and after suffering and wondering for 11 years, have only begun to find out that I even had a right to ask about my daughter. I subsequently married the father and now have an 8½-year-old little boy, who ironically enough is my daughter's brother, so you can see how I can look at my son and feel so guilty that I didn't do things right. Thinking there might be a possibility of seeing my daughter someday seems like a dream come true.

L.C., Pennsylvania

The following is from a birthmother who has been unable to have any more children though 12 years have passed. She, too, is an example of many who either never marry or ever have other children.

> I want you to know that I feel much better since I found C.U.B. I have held my secret inside of me for 12 years and even though it hurts to let it out, I have begun to feel a great relief. My husband and I have

been talking about adopting – something that I would never even think about until a couple of weeks ago. I know I'm taking on a lot all at once, but I've been living in hell for 12 years and I want out. I just hope that I can get through everything emotionally. I'm so worn out by all the circumstances of my life. Thank you so much for your help and concern.

C.J., Pennsylvania

This letter is from a grandmother who was searching for her "birth" grandchildren and just recently found them:

You may close your files on the search for my grandchildren, as I found them today. I just want you to know that after speaking to the adoptive father on the phone, I learned that correct adoption procedures as listed in the Florida Adoptions Act were not followed and false and misleading information was given to the agency. The facts of this adoption clearly point to the need for a follow-up after the adoption is finalized. I intend to help any adoptees who may need help and support them in their search for their roots.

S.R., New York

From a very frustrated mother who knew none of the details surrounding her child's adoption:

My birthdaughter will only be eight years old in November, and I realize there isn't much I can do for another ten years, but I need to know what happened. It's as though my having that baby was only a dream; like it never really happened. I don't know how it was handled, if it was ever finalized, or even if my baby lived long enough to be adopted! I was told that my life and my baby's was, for a time, very much in danger. The information I am asking for is something I should have known at the time but was never told. Is it wrong to ask who handled the legalities of the adoption? Do I have to pay for my mistake for another ten years not knowing if my baby's adoption was handled in a proper way?

D.C., Philadelphia

Many, like the following, wanted to know how they too, could become involved in the "cause":

Having given a child up for adoption 18 years ago, I realize the veracity of an organized support system such as C.U.B. for birthparents who may still be carrying an emotional burden. Please let me know how I can become involved in the organization. Thank you for your concern.

C.L., Georgia

From an adoptee:

It's such an encouragement and relief to know that many birthparents are as concerned about their "birthchildren" as we are of them! When I found out about C.U.B., it occurred to me that my natural mother may be a member. Please help me if you can. It would unlock a 22-year-old secret. God bless you for caring!

E.R., Indiana

From another adoptee — age 31 — the median age for inquiry:

As an adult adoptee, searching for her birthparents, I applaud your organization. I would be interested in any material you would be able to send me regarding your organization and any search techniques that are effective. Do you have any information available on the legal rights of adult adoptees to their records in light of last year's court decision on this subject in New Jersey? Thank you for your organization and for caring.

R.B., Connecticut

This letter was written by a birthmother to the father of her child who had been unaware of her pregnancy. Now, 15 years later, she feels the need to contact him. The letter is self-explanatory as to her reasons:

Due to the very personal nature of this letter, I am having it hand-delivered to you personally at your place of employment.

When I ended our relationship in early January, 1964, and went back home to South Jersey, I never told you the real truth as to why I was leaving. The truth was that I was pregnant by you. At the time I felt it best not to tell you. I was very upset. You were just home from the service and neither one of us were financially able to be on our own. I knew we would have to depend on our families to survive, and

129

I didn't want that for myself or for my child. I also felt unsure of how strong your affection was for me. I was afraid I would not have your full support — and too, I was afraid of how your family would respond to my pregnancy. Emotionally, I had trouble myself adjusting to the news and I sincerely felt I could not handle any type of confusion — from anyone. All I wanted to do was to go somewhere and hide. Now, after all these years my reasons for not telling you at the time all seem so meaningless.

After leaving North Jersey I contacted an adoption agency and made arrangements to go out of town and have my child quietly. I left my home in April of that year. You had telephoned me a few times from January thru April. I purposely discouraged any visits from you. I was growing heavier and I didn't want you to see me. Seeing you I might have weakened and told you the truth; by not seeing you, I felt I was able to think more clearly. Since I was pregnant and unmarried, I thought it would be best for me to surrender my child through this agency. For many reasons I would not — and could not take my child home. My daughter was born in late summer of 1964. I was alone — among strangers — in a city unfamiliar to me. Shortly after her birth I signed the final surrender papers; but I have never been able to make that same surrender in my heart.

The advice given to me by the agency was to close the door on the past year and begin a new life for myself. In time — I would forget this child. But I couldn't forget. My love and concern for her increased within me — my heart ached for her. I knew I could never forget this child — my child — I had conceived and carried. The full impact of surrender did not come as I signed the final papers; it came as I tried to rebuild my life without my child. In the beginning of my pregnancy I felt I was strong enough to handle the situation myself — but as time went by I no longer had the strength or courage that I had started out with. The first few years of adjusting to life without my child were almost unbearable for me. I have been emotionally tormented over the years for having surrendered — and for not telling you of your child. Only a few members of my own family know of my child — and they have been of very little comfort to me over the years.

About three years ago in a South Jersey newspaper a series of articles began on the adoption system. Organizations were forming for birth-parents, adoptees and adoptive parents. I joined as many as I could to enable me to learn more about adoption. What I know today I should have known then. My agency told me very little and I asked little. It was a shock to me to learn of all the emotional problems and insecurities that adoptees have. I never intended to bring these kinds of problems to my own child. My main concern for her was that she have a happy and secure home with a mother and father both. It is of great comfort to me to have learned that most adoptees have a strong desire to find and meet their birthparents. For now – I have hope that someday I will meet my daughter. This is the primary purpose of my letter to you. There is a strong possibility that when my daughter reaches the age of 18, she may return to the agency from which she was adopted and request information on her birthparents. Also, she may choose to find us herself. I am very concerned that my daughter will search and find you first. And as of this writing, you are unaware of her existence.

I have no wish to interfere with your life now or to create any problems for you or for your family. I have spared you all obligations to me and to your child. You have no idea of the emotional trauma that accompanies carrying and surrendering a child. I will never be at peace with myself until I know if she is alive and well – and if her life has been happy. All I'm asking of you now is – if she should find you first, that you send her to me. Under law you have no responsibility to either of us – but in the end I feel that you will have to answer for her creation as well as I.

I recently returned to the agency where I surrendered my child. I gave my permission to give my daughter all information I gave to them regarding her biological background – should she ever request it.

I want you to know – after you have had some time to adjust to the news of this letter that I would be available to you to discuss OUR daughter further.

Sincerely,

In conclusion of this chapter, this letter brought warmth and tears to me as well as the reason I continue to work on a volunteer basis toward adoption changes:

Dear Sandy:

I wanted to write to tell you I heard from my son.

He was so warm and receptive – I can't believe it. He told me he loved me and thanked me for giving him life and for the courage to search for him. He always knew he was adopted. He kept saying – you don't know what this means to me. We are going to meet, when I don't know yet, but we are exchanging pictures.

I am so happy, I now feel whole again. He has an adopted sister who belongs to ALMA (Adoptees Liberty Movement Assoc.) and is searching

131

for her parents in Pennsylvania. He was going to start searching but wanted to wait until he moved out of his parents' home because he didn't want to upset his mother.

Thank you for all your support.

C.F., Altoona

Yes, I reiterate — it's worth the time, the money, the effort to see one birthparent at peace with herself at finding her lost "child".

Section IV — To God Be The Glory!

*On these two commandments
hang all the law and the prophets —*

*Love the Lord thy God with all
your heart, and mind, and soul
and love your neighbor as yourself.*

— Jesus Christ

To God Be The Glory

As I worked on this adoption manuscript and reviewed my Christian experience, many parallels began to surface. There are times when our earthly experiences make clear spiritual truths that were not evident before. In this chapter, I am going to share just a few which have been especially meaningful to me.

For those of you who are unfamiliar with the story of the adulterous woman, let me share it briefly. "While Jesus was talking, the Jewish leaders and Pharisees brought a woman caught in adultery and placed her out in front of the staring crowd. They said to Jesus '... Moses in the law commanded us, that such should be stoned: but what sayest thou?' (St. John 8:5). They were trying to trap him into saying something they could use against him, but Jesus stooped down and wrote in the dust with his finger as though he had not even heard them. They kept demanding an answer, so finally he stood up and said '... He that is without sin among you, let him first cast a stone at her.' (St. John 8:7). Wow! Did that put them in their place! One by one, they slipped away. 'When Jesus had lifted up himself, and saw none but the woman, he said unto her, Woman, where are those thine accusers? hath no man condemned thee? She said, No man, Lord. And Jesus said unto her, Neither do I condemn thee: go, and sin no more.' (St. John 8:10,11)."

It began to dawn on me recently that God does not weigh sin. The commandments were given as a guideline for us to follow. As I pondered upon that, I realized that in God's eyes, infractions of commandment seven (adultery) are no worse than infractions of commandment one (you should have no other Gods; i.e. money, material good, etc.) or three (using the Lord's name in vain). Finally,

135

the point hit home that we're all guilty (which is why no one could cast the first stone!). None of us are free from condemnation. The laws of God are written on our hearts though we may have never read them or heard them.

So what is the solution? Certainly I have felt the weight of guilt. I've known the rejection of an earthly father, the loss of a child, the pain of a broken home. Whether my guilt for these things was justified or not, it was still a heavy burden for me – until nine years ago when a friend, sent by God, came along and said "I'll take your guilt – I'll carry your burden – lean on me – I will never leave you or forsake you – trust me – my grace is sufficient." He was able to make all those statements because He was perfect. He had no sin, but He was willing to take on mine so that I could be free from playing the blame game. The guilt was removed – forgiveness had been freely given. I need not justify my actions or play the blame game anymore.

There is no "pat" answer to any given situation or problem, but there is a person who is faithful and unchanging. Perhaps you who are reading this page have never really experienced the closeness of the living God. Perhaps you've never been certain of the constancy of His faithfulness. I can only tell you that when I finally "surrendered" to Him, a new way of life began. My old attitudes passed away and a new love for people which I had never before experienced took their place.

In Rod McKuen's book, *Finding My Father*, he states "I do believe that all of us are searching for the Father of us all. I intend to keep looking. I imagine you do, too". Well, my search for the Father has ended. It ended when I allowed Jesus Christ to become an intermediary between myself and my Creator – the One who "... formed me from the womb" (Isaiah 44:2) the searcher of my heart who knows everything about me. Like the adoptee, I was unsure about meeting my Father. Would He accept me? Would He like me? What kind of a relationship would we have? With all my questions and hesitancy, my intermediary friend kept nudging me on. He showed me over and over in His word that by going through Him (Jesus), (Acts 4:12) I could know the Father on a personal basis instead of in an abstract way. When I had all the pieces of the puzzle put together, my search was completed. I had been adopted into the family of God.

As I dug into the scriptures I noted how much alike the adoption procedures were then and now. In Old Testament days an adopted son received the inheritance of his adoptive family. Legally he had the same rights as that of the natural child. From a spiritual angle,

Israel is described as a son of God. The Jew is the "chosen" one (Psalms 105:6). (Could that be where the "chosen" baby story came from?) In the New Testament we see that the gentiles were grafted (adopted) in as sons (Galatians 4:5). Thus he is treated as a natural son with all the divine inheritance of the Jew at his disposal.

Something interesting came to my mind at this point. However complete in status this adoption may be — we have yet to be delivered from the bondage of our body. Possibly it is this bondage which drives an adoptee on to search out their original donor of life. As in the spiritual sense we are not totally free until we are released from this body (Romans 9:23), so an adoptee is not free until they know from whom they came — until they are able to make a connection.

We are all incomplete until we get to know the Giver of Life. This statement is true in the physical sense as well as the spiritual. Knowing one's heritage is important to one's total well-being.

We are told that the angels in heaven rejoice when just one of us are reconciled to the Father (Luke 15:7). How we in the triangle rejoice with one another when someone traces their bloodline and touches home base! The analogies go on and on. It would take the contents of another book to share them all with you. The thought excites me and is now in the process of being conceived.

If you've read this far, you are probably convinced that I am a religious "nut". Actually, what happened was that I gave up religion in exchange for Christianity. Religion is, and always has been, man's attempt to reach and please God through his own efforts. Christianity is simply God reaching down to man in the person of Jesus Christ and reconciling him back unto himself (II Corinthians 5:18).

There may come a time in your search when you find it absolutely necessary to use an intermediary. There may be no other way for you to make contact and so you choose to go that route. That was my experience in my search for God — Jesus was my intermediary (I Timothy 2:15).

We search for the "way", we discuss what "truth" is and we question what "life" is all about. Jesus summed it up in one sentence when he said "I am *the* Way, I am *the* Truth, and I am *the* Life" (John 14:6). Yes, He is all those things. My "roots" are in Him.

As I floundered through life, I felt much like the adoptee. I needed someone to link myself to so that my existence would make some sense. Without going into a long dissertation, a brief illustration of an oak and a telephone pole will help to explain what I mean.

As you walk down almost any street, you will see large, leafy arms across the street forming a beautiful canopy of green. In between

137

the oaks are large, weatherbeaten, splintered, telephone poles. Although they stand as erect as the oaks, they sprout no branches, shoot forth no leaves and contribute nothing to the beauty and symphony of the greenery. What is it that makes the difference? It is this. The oaks have roots and the telephone poles have none. A Christian becomes like an oak. He sinks his roots deep down into the promises of God, and in those promises is found the source of transforming life (Ephesians 3:17).

The most important thing to happen at the end of a search is to possess the knowledge of one's true identity. That is the same reason we are constantly in search of God. We are not at peace until we find our rest in our Creator — the one who gave us life! If you are still searching, I can give you a good lead. You will find Him at the foot of the cross. He'll meet you there!

To God be the glory for the completion of this book. It was a dual endeavor. He planted the seed in my fertile mind; it was watered by my tears and began to grow as I delved back into the past and brought forth old hurts; the encouraging words of my family and friends were used to cultivate it; and finally the power and warmth of the Son brought it to fruition.

May its pages be an encouragement and a reminder that you are not alone. Keep asking, keep seeking, and keep knocking. You will receive, you will find, and the doors will be opened to you.

Postscript

A year has just recently passed since I met my daughter for the first time. Her birthday was only a few weeks ago. Due to the circumstances, I debated about sending her a card, but it wasn't long before I realized that I just couldn't let it go by. Especially, not after all those years of wanting to send one and being unable to do so.

I went to a bookstore where I purchase Sunday School supplies and as I began to look through the cards, I called on my closest friend to help me. I mean after all — what kind of a card do you send to someone in this situation? A special friend card? She's so much more than that! A card to a daughter for all the years of joy she's brought? Impossible. Just a plain daughter card? Too presumptuous.

"Lord", I said, "I need a card that's just right!" No sooner had I uttered the words that a card stood out from all the others on the rack and it was the only one of its kind! It said it all. On the outside of the card was a beautiful rose and over the rose it said "You'll never know...". The inside said "how many times I've wished for you a Happy Birthday." That was it! How perfect — it fit so well.

To the adoptees who are searching — from the birthparents who are anxiously awaiting your arrival, may I say on behalf of them all — "You'll never know...how many times we've wished for you a Happy Birthday."

I Would Have Searched Forever

An Open Letter to the Daughter I Surrendered, but Never Forgot — Isaiah 49:15

The day you were born was a hot summer day — July always is. It was a Sunday morning — Sunday's child is full of grace — at 11:45 a.m. All over the country praises were being sung as you came bounding into the world.

The year was 1954. A few days following your arrival, you and I would part — they said, forever. Strange how times have changed. We were victims of circumstances. The plain fact was that you had to go live with other parents because this mother, though she was capable of giving you life, was incapable of giving you anything else — except love. They said that wasn't enough.

I was hurt to think that they would not even permit me to gaze upon you — you the child of my womb;[1] the child I had grown attached to during those nine months; the months you grew inside and became a very part of my being.

But I was only 15. They said, I would forget.[2] I would have other children; I would start a new life and I would close the door on this chapter of my life. I did have other children. I did start a new life, but no — I never forgot and I never closed the door. It was always ajar. During the nights filled with tears,[3] I could not comprehend a loving God allowing me to go through a whole lifetime and never know you.

They placed you in a new home. They told you that you were adopted. You loved those who were truly your parents. But all that did not change the fact that you and I would someday have a longing down deep within us to know one another. Though our fates had separated us, we shared a bond that no legal document could change.

The price was high — a child I could never see — imposed secrecy — the scarlet letter emblazoned upon my soul. I gave you life, but you gave me hope. The lessons learned, the wisdom gained, the growth acquired has all been immeasurable.[4]

I search for you. I find you. I learn that you, too, had been searching for me. I tell you of my love and the years I longed to know you — and then again I release you. Thank you for allowing me to know you. The truth has set me free. I am a new person because we've touched.

Sandy Musser

Scriptural References:
[1] Psalm 139:13   [3] Psalm 126:5
[2] Isaiah 49:15   [4] James 3:17

140

The Rest Of The Story

The pages you have just read comprised the original version of I WOULD HAVE SEARCHED FOREVER. In this 5th printing, a few excerpts from my second book, WHAT KIND OF LOVE IS THIS, are included so that you, the reader, can know "the rest of the story"!

A New Year and New Relationships

Winter flew by. Early in May, 1980, I attended the second national adoption conference held in Anaheim, CA, which represented 200 grass-root groups joined in pursuit of open adoption records.

It was during that week I had an opportunity to reconcile unresolved feelings with my ex-husband. He had moved from our home in NJ to CA following our divorce and was not far from Anaheim. We met together and communicated in a way we had been unable to do during our entire 20 year marriage! Why?

Did opening the closet door and finally dealing with the "secret" enable me to relate differently? Was my new self-esteem in operation? Was he more comfortable with the person I had become since finding my daughter? Was I a more self-assured, confident individual than I had been during our marriage?

We now share a unique friendship. Though we are reconciled, we are not together. Reconciliation simply means to restore to friendship and a lack of enmity. We hold no grudges, bitterness, or anger toward one another. Each of us has accepted our share of responsibility for the failure of our marriage — we have grown.

141

I believe that the marriage might have been saved if I could have resolved the adoption issue much earlier. Being forced, by societal pressure, to remain in the closet made me feel that I was not a worthwhile person. As a result I became a jealous, possessive wife, fearful of losing the person I loved — just as I had lost my daughter. It was a wonderful feeling to be able to discuss these things openly with the man whom I had spent half my life.

That fall I was invited to speak to an adoptive parents' group in San Antonio, Texas, sponsored by Lutheran Social Services and the Council on Adoptable Children. They were having a "reunion" banquet for parents who had adopted children through their agency. I was honored by their invitation and, as a birthmother, considered it a rare opportunity. It was to become one of the highlights of my speaking engagements.

I marveled at their warm acceptance. They weren't threatened by my presence, nor were they hostile (as other adoptive parent groups had been). Certainly they were a unique group. As I began to talk with Kathleen Silber, the director of the agency, I understood why. They operated from a totally different perspective than the 'traditional' agencies. Openness was not only encouraged, but also emphasized. Regular meetings of birthparents and adoptive parents and an exchange of letters between the parties was the norm. It was routine. Tearing down walls and building bridges was apparently their mission.

An adoptive mother approached me following the meeting and expressed the love she felt for her son's birthmother since communicating with her by letter. She also said she has a strong desire to meet her and invite her into her home. That's what real caring is all about! When we finally begin to communicate with one another, we realize that we're not adversaries at all; though the courts and agencies see us as such.

Two weeks following the meeting in San Antonio, I was asked to lead a panel of birthparents at the Southeastern Regional Conference in Atlanta, GA. The topic to be discussed was "The Birthparent Dilemma". In my closing remarks that day I mentioned that although Wendy and I had not had a relationship for the past three years, I firmly believed that someday we would. I never lost faith that the day would come when my daughter and I would once again be "reunited". But, I can assure you, I never dreamed it would be only four days later!

On October 8, 1980 at 9:32 p.m., Wendy called. Would I come to dinner Saturday evening? WOULD I? Without her saying so, it was obvious to me that she wanted a reconciliation. That week-end she told me that she had reached the lowest point in her life — and needed to connect with me. She couldn't have paid me a greater compliment.

I had always kept the door open. During that three year dry-spell I faithfully sent her a birthday card, a Christmas card, and an occasional letter. She said that my keeping in touch did make it easier for her to reconnect when she was ready to do so.

The following week I called to see if she might want to attend a conference in Virginia Beach. Fortunately for me, Virginia Beach was one of her favorite resort spots. Three weeks after her initial call, we attended the Mid-Atlantic Regional Conference and shared our ups and downs with those present. Again, the experience was beyond my wildest dream. We had lots of time to discuss our feelings openly and honestly. It was the beginning of our new relationship — a relationship that is blossoming to this present day.

The message of the Prodigal Son parable is not only of the returning son, but also the father's open arms — waiting to welcome his child back. I waited with open arms and I believed — and I welcomed my child back!

In February, 1981, Wendy, her adoptive mother, and I had the pleasure of being guests on the CBN 700 Club. Our appearance together conveyed to those watching that agape love brings acceptance. We were grateful for the chance to share our experience and in some small way reach out and touch the lives of many.

The Ultimate Reunion

June 29, 1981, marked another milestone in my emotional healing. That was the day I met with the birthfather for the first time in twenty-eight years. I had not seen or talked to him since high school.

The American Adoption Conference in 1981 was held in Kansas City, MO. Many unresolved feelings were brought to the surface that I didn't even realize were buried. Though I had been active in the movement for five years, I still had not begun to deal on an emotional level. The 1982 conference in San Antonio awakened those feelings even more and began a process within me that I could no longer control.

143

The stark, harsh realty that I would never — and could never — know my daughter as a child suddenly surfaced as I watched a slide presentation of young children and moms — and listened to a correlated music tape. Intellectually I knew that those years were gone forever, but the impact struck me that day like a ton of bricks — and what followed was a flood of tears — tears that had not been shed since I left the hospital in 1954.

Painful? Absolutely! But finally healing was on its way. Like physical healing, emotional healing for some of us takes longer than for others. There will always be a scar and though a scar doesn't hurt, it is a reminder of the pain once suffered.

A few days following the conference in San Antonio, I decided to contact the birthfather. I believed that my mental health was at stake. When I expressed my need to talk about the manner in which our relationship had ended, he agreed, without hesitation, to meet with me. We also made arrangements for him to meet his daughter for the first time.

We had decided to meet for lunch at a restaurant close to my home. As the time drew closer, I began to get butterflies thinking about how it would feel to see him after 28 years. Is it true that you never forget your "first love"? We arrived at the restaurant almost simultaneously. As he walked toward me, I thought my heart would drop to my feet. I felt as though I were 15 years old again and it was 1954. Yes — I believe it's true — you never forget your 'first love'.

We spent several hours sharing our past and present lives. He said that over the years he would justify his actions to himself by thinking "There was nothing you could have done — you were only fifteen". But then he went on, "There was something I could have done, but I was a coward. I could have given you emotional support. I could have 'been there' for you and I wasn't. All I can say is — I'm sorry".

"I'm sorry" was music to my ears. It was obviously what I needed to hear because 28 years of hurt melted away. Ridiculous, you say. Maybe. All I know is that the burden I carried alone for those 28 years lifted when I heard him speak those few little works, and the sincerity with which they were spoken.

We left the restaurant and drove to Wendy's home. She greeted her birthfather with a big hug which was reciprocal. After a short time I offered to take my 5 year old "adopted" grandson out for a treat so that Wendy and her birthfather could have some time alone.

Upon my return, the three of us spent a few hours chit-chatting, laughing, and taking pictures. I was amazed at how comfortable it felt.

I arrived back home around midnight and as I walked in the door, the phone was ringing. It was Wendy. She just wanted to thank me for putting the last piece in her puzzle — and thank me she did. She was extremely happy to finally meet her birthfather.

I know that I'm speaking on behalf of all of us when I say that there are no words to properly describe the feeling of wholeness that comes from such an encounter. I can only wish it for everyone. Our smiling faces, shining forth from the pictures we took, give a glowing memory of that day in June when the three of us came together for a healing reunion.

Mission accomplished!

Parables

"He who has ears, let him hear" - Matt. 11:15

The following section of parables and spiritual analogies are included especially for those in the Christian community or anyone else with spiritual thoughts and leanings.

Parables of Reconciliation

Reconciliation parables permeate the scriptures. In fact, reconciliation is always the "bottom-line" purpose of every religion. From Moses longing for and defending his own kin to Joseph being reunited with his brothers; from the parable of the lost sheep to the parable of the lost coin; from the return of the prodigal son — to the angels in heaven rejoicing over one returning soul.

The following parables offer terrific analogies to those of us in the adoption triangle who want so desperately to be reunited and reconciled with our missing loved ones. See if you don't agree.

Most of us at one time or another have heard the story of the 100 sheep and the one which got lost. Though 99 were left, the missing one was constantly being sought. This comes from the parable of the shepherd counting his sheep at the close of each day to make sure none had strayed. If one was missing, he searched for it immediately. Not only did he track down the missing sheep, but he made direct contact with it. He picked it up in his arms and returned it to the fold. The scripture uses the phrase "to go after" which conveys persistence and success. When he found it, he calls together his friends and neighbors and says "Rejoice with me; for I have found my sheep which was lost." (Luke 15:4)

REJOICE WITH ME — I HAVE FOUND MY DAUGHTER
WHICH I HAD LOST!

Since coins were more scarce in Palestine than in modern civilization, they often represented the savings of many years. In this parable a woman is about to sweep her house clean in order to find one lost coin — even though she had nine others. All her energies are put into this search. She lights a candle for the express purpose of having the light shine in order for her to find it. The broom used for other purposes now sweeps only to find the missing coin. Her two eyes look for nothing else. Her candle, her broom, her eyesight, her body limbs, her faculties of mind are all employed in searching for her lost treasure (Luke 15:8).

WITH MY BODY, SOUL AND SPIRIT, I SEARCHED FOR
MY LOST TREASURE — AND FOUND HER!

The next parable popularly known as the Prodigal Son could appropriately be called The Father's Open Arms. Though many years had separated them and the son was no longer a part of the family circle, the father was constantly watching for the return of his boy. We are told that when the father saw him coming, he reserved the best robe (always reserved for an honored guest) and a ring (which marked the position of sonship). A feast was immediately held. The fatted calf was the animal held in readiness for a special occasion. The return of his son was the cause for a major celebration. Take note of the reaction of the son who had remained with him. It was one of extreme jealousy. He was angry over what he regarded as an injustice when he expressed, "All these many years have I served you!" The language implies self-righteousness, self-pity, and an inward alienation from his father. The father then reminds him that he has always been with him, and all that he has is his — "but this your brother was dead, and is alive again; and was lost and is found." (Luke 15:11)

SHE'S ALIVE — SHE'S ALIVE!
MY DAUGHTER IS ALIVE!

147

I believe that these parables confirm that God is as interested in physical reconciliations as He is in spiritual ones.

Does God Care About Genealogy?

Genealogy has been given a prominent place in the Bible. One does not have to look very far before finding lots and lots of begats: Abraham begat Isaac, Isaac begat Jacob, and so on. The genealogy of Moses is presented in Exodus 6:14-20 in which his birthparents are named (no sealed record here!).

In the first chapter of the New Testament, the genealogy of Jesus is recorded for the express purpose of proving that he was a descendent of the House of David. Had he been unable to trace his Jewish heritage back to the House of David — he could not have claimed to be the Son of God.

Additional food for thought — where might all of Christendom be if 15 year old Mary had been forced into giving up Baby Jesus under the present day closed system of adoption — unable to trace his Jewish heritage — we could not have accepted his claim as the Son of God!

Yes, there is no doubt about it. Genealogy is so important to God that His written word exclaims the genealogy of generation after generation — until we arrive at the 20th century when man decided to redo history by performing closed adoptions and then sealing those records "forever".

There is a verse in scripture that states "I have seen their affliction and heard their cries". I am convinced that He has heard our cries and is responding. Hundreds of reunions and reconciliations are taking place daily in spite of the "impenetrable" sealed documents. Those of us who suffer from the injustices of a system that separates and denies individuals their God-given right to roots are glad to know that "our cries are being heard".

What's In A Name?

In Rollo May's book Man's Search for Himself, he makes a profound statement concerning this very question. He states:

"Let us remind ourselves that after all, the experience of one's own identity, or becoming a person, is the simplest experience in life even though at the same time the most profound. As everyone knows, a little child will react indignantly and strongly if you, in teasing, call him by the wrong name. It is as though you take away his identity — a most precious thing to him. In the Old Testament the phrase 'I will blot out their names' — to erase their identity and it will be as though they never had existed — is a more powerful threat than physical death."

Our names are very precious to all of us. The fact that given birth names are changed when an adoption placement takes place seems unfair and unjust. Who among us would want the name our mother had given us changed upon will. Were we able to cry out, we would probably say "Stop — this is the name my mother chose for me!"

As Open Adoption is becoming more and more prevalent, so too is the choosing of the name by the birthparent(s) and adoptive parents together.

Familiar Sounding Lingo

I am always astonished how much of our adoption "lingo" is like that of the scriptures. For instance: The words "chosen" and "rejected" are used repeatedly. The inference is that the Jews were the "chosen" but since they "rejected" the Messiah, the gentiles were grafted (adopted) in making them the "chosen" sons of God (via adoption). Interesting, don't you think?

In Exodus 4:22 the Lord is talking to Moses and telling him to tell Pharaoh that "Israel is my son, even my firstborn". It goes on to explain how the Israelites became scattered — "My sheep wandered through all the mountains and upon every hill; you, my flock were scattered upon all the face of the earth." But then it goes on to point out how God's plan for His people was and still is reconciliation when He said, "Behold I, even I, will both search my sheep and seek them out". (Ezek. 34:11)

JUST AS WE SEARCH FOR AND SEEK OUT
OUR CHILDREN AND PARENTS!

Jesus Christ, the promised Messiah, became a stumbling block to the Jewish people. He had paved the way for them to enjoy the fruit of salvation, which was something they were unable to do on their own. Are birthparents stumbling blocks to adoptive parents — since the birthparent made possible what was otherwise impossible. An infertile parent can not enjoy the benefit of parenting apart from the woman who gives birth and is willing to sacrifice her own flesh and blood.

Another oft-used term is the word "intermediary" Jesus is referred to as the intermediary — the only way to the Father. Likewise, many of us have found someone who became our intermediary, paving the way for us to meet the special person we had been seeking.

The Trinity and The Triangle

Those of us raised in the Christian faith are very familiar with the concept of the trinity consisting of three persons in one — the Father, Son and Holy Spirit. These three make up what is known as the Godhead. These three persons actually have three separate roles while remaining one complete unit.

How alike is the adoption triangle! Three separate parts, but one unit — a unit intricately knit into one whole. The birthparents gave their heredity; the adoptive parents provided the environment; and finally, the adoptee, benefiting from both "real" parents become their own unique person.

Each fulfills his own role. No one in the triangle thinks their position is more important than the other. Each one realizes and understands that the other does not negate not detract from their own particular function.

Throughout scripture the Father, Son and Holy Spirit are depicted as giving glory and praise to one another. What an example for us in the Triangle! The majority of birthparents I have met and talked with always give praise and gratefulness to the adoptive parents of the child they "surrendered". Most adoptive parents are appreciative to the birthparents for giving them 'the gift of life'. (But, sadly, many more feel threatened). Adoptees benefiting from both "real" parents usually (not always) have much to be thankful for.

We have been bound together and may not even understand why, but we need not fear one another. His love casts out fear (I John 4:18). He has not given us a spirit of fear, but of power and love. (II Tim. 1:7)

Called To Be A Deliverer

Jochebed was the mother of Moses. At the time she gave birth to him, the Pharoah had issued an order to midwives to kill all Hebrew male children at birth. Though Moses had a natural birth, the fact that he survived and grew up when all male Hebrew children were being destroyed is noteworthy.

How Jochebed managed to save her son during the first three months of Moses' life is not recorded. But when he became three months old, she decided upon a plan of leaving her baby in a handmade ark. (Today this would be considered abandonment, but notice how this mother is planning her child's placement!)

With the help of her daughter, Miriam, she laid her baby among the papyrus reeds near the river's bank and left Miriam to watch over him. She knew that Pharoah's daughter was accustomed to bathing at this spot. Pharoah's daughter appeared with her maidens and came upon the ark. She heard the whimpering child and said "This is one of the Hebrews' children". (Exodus 2:6)

Young Miriam, standing close by said, "Shall I go and call a nurse of the Hebrew women, that she may nurse the child for you? And Pharoah's daughter replied "Go"! (And the first open adoption was about to be initiated). So it was that Jochebed received the joyful news that she could nurse her own child.

Though Moses was soon adopted by Pharoah's daughter, it was his own mother who would watch over him as a small child. It was she who instilled in him a belief in God. It was she who imparted the sacred traditions of Israel and who told him of the divine promise to Abraham and his decendents — that they would become a great nation.

Yet this unassuming Levite mother could rejoice that her son, Moses, as the adopted son of the princess, received the best education of the highest order. She undoubtedly had an inward joy as she watched her son grow into manhood. In later years, Moses would remember his mother's God and the faith she had in Him. He would remain a Hebrew all the years of his life.

The scripture says that when Moses became a man, he went out among his own bretheren and lifted their burden. God had placed him in a unique position. He had been called to set his people free, but he was not a willing subject. In fact, he made all kinds of excuses as to why he was not the man for the job. He questioned God by asking "Who am I, that I should go to Pharoah and that I should bring forth the children of Lsrael out of Egypt?" And each time the Lord answered, Moses had another excuse ready.

First he insisted that they wouldn't believe him; then he said that he was not an eloquest speaker. The Lord responded "Who has made man's mouth . . . Go therefore and I will teach you what you should say." (Exodus 4:11) As the story progresses, we see that Moses gains more and more courage and finally takes his proper place as leader.

I share the above to draw an analogy to those of us in the adoption reform movement. Moses' people were in physical bondage. Our people are in mental bondage — psychological and emotional — stripped of their entire bloodline. There is no question that we need more leaders, like Moses, willing to speak on behalf of adoptees, birthparents, adoptive parents, siblings and all others separated from their families of origin. Individuals all over the country are being kept in bondage by their "taskmasters" (the courts, the agencies, the system)!

Along with others, I have accepted the challenge, but not without giving many of the same excuses which Moses gave. Over the years, I've gained more and more courage and am now fully committed to the work of reuniting separated loved ones as well as questioning the powers to be concerning this issue of stolen birthrights.

What Can You Do?

When you've been set free by a completed search, settled your "adoption experience" or just believe in basic rights, it should be your privilege, your honor and your duty to help someone else become free. Please join me in this challenge — the challenge to set our people free. If your answer is yes, then will you also have a share in my dream?

My dream is to create a retreat center where searchers can come to spend as much time as they need learning the "how to" of search techniques. All kinds of research material would be available.

It would be a safe place for girls and women with "untimely" pregnancies to come and find solace, without pressure, while examining their alternatives.

It would be a place for perspective adoptive parents to learn about open adoption and consider it as a viable choice — only after dealing with their infertility issues.

It would be a place for professionals to come to study the concepts and theories of open adoption and receive training from open adoption leaders.

It would be a place where seminars and workshops would be held on a regular basis — both in-house and around the country. These Encounter Seminars would deal with all aspects of loss, separation, reunification and reconciliation.

It would be a place of learning and could be called Adoption Educational Institute for Openness and Understanding (AEIOU). It would be a clearinghouse for the child welfare system.

If you believe that such a place can be created, if you believe it would be a worthwhile project, and if you have something to offer by way of property, facililities, services, or just ideas for establishing, supporting and maintaining such an operation, please feel free to write or call — and let's discuss it.

Maybe together we can turn this dream into reality — so that the day will finally come when NO ONE will ever have to go "in search" because openness will be the law of the land! Is it possible?

Write to me in care of:
The Musser Foundation
P. O. Box 1860
Cape Coral, FL 33910
813-542-1342

In closing — I want to share that I am at a much different place spiritually than I was when I first wrote I WOULD HAVE SEARCHED FOREVER in 1978. But I still believe that each of us has to make peace with our Higher Power within — whatever we choose to call Him. And I believe that when you've been reconciled with your Higher Power, then you'll know within your spirit that reconciliation is what He desires and wants for all His children. And that NO ONE has the right to deny you the opportunity to be reunited with your missing loved ones — not the State, not the Court, not the Agency or anyone else. So go for it! It will change your life!

I Would Have Searched Forever

THE SUPREME SACRIFICE

God, something occurred to me recently as I was thinking about the child I had to surrender years ago. I recall that you, too, gave up Your child. I've studied in Your Word how painful that was and what a great sacrifice — to give up Your Son. Apparently there was no other way. or You would have found it.[1]

You know, Lord, I also gave up my child. There was no other way either. But I am comforted in knowing that You have walked in my footsteps and understand my heartache.

You were reconciled with You Son, Lord, but they tell me I have no right to be reconciled with mine. Since Your Son was brought into the world for the express purpose of reconciliation[2] — could it be that my child might accomplish that same end — bringing together two sets of parents, siblings and other extended family members who love him?

Wasn't that Your ultimate goal when You made the decision to make the Supreme Sacrifice[3] — to reconcile us to one another, to teach us how to love and thereby draw us closer to You?

Lord, if those of us who are intimately involved in the adoption triangle can accomplish that goal, then the Supreme Sacrifice will not have been in vain — neither Yours not mine.

An Aching Birthmother

[1]Isaiah 53   [2]2Corinthians 5:19   [3]John 1:29

National Organizations

The Musser Foundation
P.O. Box 1860
Cape Coral, FL 33910
813-542-1342 / Fax 813-549-9393

Adoption & Family Reunion Ctr.
1105 Cape Coral Parkway
Cape Coral, FL 33904
813-542-1342

Concerned United Birthparents
2000 Walker Street
Des Moines, IA 50317
515-263-9541

Adop. Parents for Open Records
P. O. Box 193
Long Valley, NJ 07853

Int'l Soundex Reunion Registry
P. O. Box 2312
Carson City, NV 89702

ALARM Network (Lobbying Org)
P. O. Box 6581
Ft. Myers, FL 33911
813-542-1785

Nat'l Org. of Birthparents
P. O. Box 1993
Baltimore, MD 21203
301-243-3986

American Adoption Congress
1000 Connecticut Ave. NW #9
Washington, D.C. 20036

Orphan Voyage
2141 Road 2300
Cedaredge, CO 81413

Americans for Open Records
P. O. Box 401
Palm Desert, CA 92261
619-341-2619

Reunions, the Magazine
P. O. Box 11727
Milwaukee, WI 53211-0727
414-263-4567

Council for Equal Rights
401 E. 74 St. Su. 17D
New, York,NY 10021
212-988-0110

TRIADOPTION®
P. O. Box 638
Westmister, CA 92684
714-892-4098

In addition to the above, there are hundreds of search/support organizations all over the country. You can quickly obtain specific referrals to organizations and individuals who specialize in search and support by dialing —

1-900-7SEARCH

To utilize your time on the line to its fullest potential, look up the area code for the areas that are most useful to your search — e.g. the city or county of birth, surrender, adoption, or where you are currently residing. It allows you constant access to current, updated referrals and you can all any time of the day or night. You can also get instructions on how to obtain other services. $2.00 per minute will be charged to your phone bill.

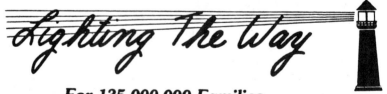

ADOPTION
AWARENESS
BOOKS

DISTRIBUTED
BY

Lighting the Way for 135,000,000 Families
Separated by Adoption

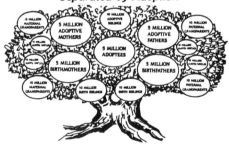

We distribute and promote the following
books as fundraisers for our organization.
Since we are constantly adding new material,
please call for information:
813-542-1342

SEARCH BOOKS

☐ **Adoption Searchbook** — *Mary Jo Rillera.*
After taking the reader through the many emotional stages of adoption, she then skillfully presents steps for conducting a search, and how to make the information work for you. $20

☐ **Faint Trails** — *Hal Aigner.* A brief, but valuable search book. A great source for locating those special repositories of information and how and where to find them. $10

☐ **How To Search In Canada** — *Joan Marshall.* An excellent resource book for anyone searching in Canada. It provides various forms for personal use. $20

☐ **The Great Adoptee Search Book** — *Jean Strauss.* A short but informative book for beginning searchers; step by step procedures are presented in a simplified manner. $12

☐ **You Can Find Anyone!** — *Eugene Ferraro.* An incredible wealth of information, ideas and resources. Become an expert by following the foolproof methods and procedures. $20

PERSONAL

☐ **An Adopted Woman** — *Katrina Maxtone-Graham.* The author states that we are victims of a system that claims to "protect", but, in fact, holds us powerless. She was determined to know the truth and unravel the mysteries that plagued her life. Hardcover $20

☐ **On The Outside Looking Inside** — *Michael Reagan.* The intimate autobiography of the adopted son of former President Ronald Reagan and Jane Wyman. A revealing story. $5

☐ **Mother, Can You Hear Me?** — *E. Cooper Allen.* The extraordinary true story of an adoptee who found her mother in a state institution after a fifty year separation. A warm and extremely touching story. Hardcover $15

☐ **Missing Links** — *Vincent Begley.* To millions of people who answer to the name of 'adoptee', adoption is both a paradox and enigma. The author takes you along on his mysterious search as he learns of his birthfather's "calling" and discovers another sibling. $10

☐ **Tangled Web** — *Jean Maddern Pitrone.* The story of the "cast-off Siamese Twin" · an alleged daughter of auto pioneer, John Dodge. A bizarre tale which allows readers to draw their own conclusions. Hardcover $20

☐ **The Other Mother** — *Carol Schaefer.* The Other Mother shares the experience of a birthmother in a most intimate way. A recommended book for anyone interested in the psychological ramifications of surrendering a child. Hardcover $25

☐ **Wanted: First Child** — *Rebecca Harsin.* A moving true story of a birthmother's plight. This book will help others to understand the pain and suffering that most birthmothers experience. $12

REFORM BOOKS

☐ **Adoption - A Handful Of Hope** — *Suzanne Arms.* The rights and lives of birthmothers and children are all too often overlooked in society's attempts to protect and judge. The author states that adoption practices will have to change $15

☐ **Adoption Encounter** — *Mary Jo Rillera.* Adoption influences the conscious and unconscious of those touches; it involves bonding, separation, loss and gain. Mary Jo an adoptee and birthparent, has a unique understanding of the entire adoption process. $20

☐ **Adoption Triangle** — *Baran, Pannor & Sorosky.* The first book to explore, evaluate, and consider the basic need for change. It clarifies the unique problems of triangle members. An excellent resource book! $10

☐ **Birthbond** — *Judi Gediman & Linda Brown.* Reunions · and What Happens After · The heart of this book centers on the in-depth interviews with thirty birthmothers. Birthbond challenges our perceptions of adoption and helps us understand maternal bonds. Pub. 1/90. Hardcover $25

☐ **Dark Side of Adoption** — *Marsha Riben.* Many whose lives have been irrevocably touched by adoption are acutely aware of the many problems inherent in the current sealed adoption system. A shocking and revealing investigative report. An excellent resource book. $15

☐ **Faces of Adoption** — *Lynn Giddens.* The author is an adoptee and Founder of AIE in N.C. She examines many relevant questions related to the adoption process and explains why adoption is not a single event but an on-going process. $8

☐ **Lost & Found** — *Betty Jean Lifton.* This powerful and eloquent book makes a plea for the right of the adopted to know their origins. B.J. Lifton, an adoptee, brings to life every stage of the psychological journey. $15

☐ **Solomon Says** — *Louise Armstrong.* An expose' of foster care. Because the realities of a failed system are evident on every page, this is not an easy book to read. But through this powerful work, Ms. Armstrong offers some answers. $10

☐ **Stolen Birthright** — *Sandra Kay Musser.* Subtitled America's Adoption Travesty, the author confronts and challenges the legal, moral and ethical issues surrounding adoption procedures and practices in America. A great resource book. Dec.'91 Pub. Date $15

☐ **The Adoption Machine** — *JoAnne Swanson.* A small, but dynamic and shocking booklet - one that tells it like it is! It summarizes the unmet needs and injustices faced by the closed, secret system, and reveals NCFA tactics. Terrific resource. **$5**

☐ **The Reunion Book** — *Mary Jo Rillera.* 70 individuals share their reunion stories. All aspects of their experience - and how they survived the separation, reunion and rebuilding process. **$20**

☐ **The Solomon Decision** — *Kate Pijanowski.* Personal interviews with members of the triad, and discussion of agencies who still practice the conspiracy of secrecy. Dr. Thomas Bouchard's study of "Twins Reared Apart" is also included. **$10**

☐ **Yes . . .But** — *Ginni Snodgrass.* Another small, but important booklet - answers the most-asked questions. If you have unanswered questions about adoption or need help responding to questions, this book will be useful. **$5**

OPEN ADOPTION

☐ **Adoption Without Fear** — Edited by *Jim Gritter.* Sixteen true stories of open adoption. Many of the contributors have shared the birth experience with the birth parents. They all found that openness gave deeper meaning to the process. **$15**

☐ **Children Of Open Adoption** — *Kathleen Silber & Patricia Dorner.* Two pioneers in the field of open adoption are now able to present important evidence that answers the question — what is the effect of open adoption on the children? **$15**

MAGAZINES

☐ **Reunions - The Magazine.** The best reunion magazine on the market! Reunions, The Magazine covers all types of reunion stories, as well as a classified section for locating your missing person. 4 issues a year. - 60 pages. **$24**

VIDEO/AUDIO

☐ **The Right To Know** 60 min. video ... **$30**

☐ **A Teddy Bear & A Rose** by Janelle .. **$5**
☐ **Child I Cannot Claim** — Diane Brown **$5**
   Music Tapes

☐ **Open My Records Day**
   Radio Interview **$5**

SPEECHES

☐ **3 Reform Speeches** — Musser **$7.50**
   I Have A Dream
   This Time Must Come
   Musings Of A Birthparent

We also carry an assortment of pins and bumper stickers. For more information call

813-542-1342

10% on 3-5 bks—15% on 6-10 bks—20% on 11-20 bks
25% on 21-35 bks—30% on 36-50 bks

☐ Adoption — A Handful of Hope $15
☐ Adoption Encounter $20
☐ Adoption Triangle $10
☐ Adoption Searchbook $20
☐ Adoption Without Fear $15
☐ An Adopted Woman $20
☐ Birthbond $25
☐ Children of Open Adoption $15
☐ Dark Side of Adoption $15
☐ Faces of Adoption $5
☐ Faint Trails $10
☐ How To Search In Canada $20
☐ Lost & Found $15
☐ Missing Links $10
☐ Mother, Can You Hear Me? $15
☐ On The Outside Looking Inside $5
☐ Solomon Says $10
☐ Stolen Birthright $15
☐ Tangled Web $20
☐ The Adoption Machine $5
☐ The Great Adoptee Search Book $12
☐ The Other Mother $25
☐ The Reunion Book $20
☐ The Solomon Decision $10
☐ Wanted: First Child $12
☐ Yes. . .But $5
☐ You Can Find Anyone $20
☐ Reunion - The Magazine $24
☐ Speeches $7.50
☐ Video $30
☐ Audio $5
                Add $1.00 postage per book
      Enclosed is a check in the amount of $ _____
Name _____

Address _____

City, State, Zip _____

Triad Status: _____ Phone: _____
              Send Check & Form to:
         The Musser Foundation
   Adoption & Family Awareness Center
   P.O. Box 1860, Cape Coral FL 33910
   Or call 813-542-1342 to place your order.